Praise for

TRULY SIGNIFICANT

"This book is one of the rare pieces of literature that makes you stop and think about your own actions during your life, and if you haven't done so before—now is the time. It's never too late to explore your own humanity; and what you have contributed back to society for the greater good."

~Scott Rivello, Retired Senior Partner, EY
Board Member, The Giannis Group

"Purpose leads us to significance. It is what drives our souls to connect with humanity through our gifts. *Truly Significant* shines a bright light on those who took bold action and became a beacon of light for others to follow."

~Sylvia Worsham, Best selling Author
In Faith, I Thrive.

"Truly Significant invites readers on a transformative journey, moving beyond success to embrace a life of service and impact. Through powerful stories of figures like Viktor Frankl and Dr. Jane Goodall, this book shows how true significance is found in serving others. It challenges us to redefine our purpose, inspiring a shift toward meaningful contributions that leave a lasting legacy in the world. Discover the strength and fulfillment in living with significance."

~Tim Love, Former Vice-Chair
Omnicom Group

"Explore these inspiring stories that are examples of finding your purpose and answering God's calling. May we all aspire to be truly significant by serving others...especially in mentoring."

~Diane Paddison, Founder of 4word
Author of *Work, Love, Pray and Be Refreshed*

"Making a difference is at the heart of what next-gen leaders crave in corporate culture—they want to build a social legacy. Check out these 40 inspiring stories of people who switched gears to help others and make our world better."

~Jane Gentry, Futurist
Founder—JaneGentry & Company

Truly Significant is a timely and inspiring guide to intentional living. With heartfelt wisdom, Rick invites readers to pause, reflect on what truly matters, and realign their lives with purpose. This book challenges the pursuit of surface-level success and instead encourages a deeper journey—one rooted in meaningful relationships, cultural empathy, and the kind of impact that outlasts us. Whether through transformative travel or everyday choices, *Truly Significant* offers a path to living a life that resonates with authenticity and lasting significance."

~Serban Maracine, CFP®

"As an Asian American, I found Emily Chang's story truly significant. She acts. I was so touched by her love for Teo. Her daughter Laini's actions in building bridges between cultures are also inspiring!"

~Qing Mu
President, Haobby, Inc.

"In *Truly Significant*, Rick weaves together personal accounts, memories, and heartfelt testimonials that remind us to value the people and moments that have shaped who we are. He touches on the influences that form our personalities, our approach to family, work, play, faith, and our generosity toward others. It is a powerful reminder that we are all products of our environments and that we should take time to appreciate the truly significant people, events, and yes, even the pets, that help define our lives."

~Martin Rowinski
Founder, Boardsi

"I really liked the way *Truly Significant* connects a sense of purpose to having significant impact. Of the many powerful stories, I especially liked the Viktor Frankel story. Viktor's quote involves "if you have a 'why' to live, you can endure any 'how.'" As the founder of the Lab for Transformative Leadership, I firmly believe that purpose is the most powerful force to tap into our personal energy source and achieve truly significant outcomes. Tocquigny does a wonderful job in this book of providing examples that are both entertaining and informative."

~Vince Gennaro
Founder, NYU Lab for Transformative Leadership

TRULY SIGNIFICANT

ALSO BY RICK TOCQUIGNY

When Core Values Are Strategic
Life Lessons
Life Lessons: For Grads . . . All Ages and Stages
Life Lessons: Simple Words That Matter
Life Lessons from Veterans
My Journal: With God All Things Are Possible
Sermon Notes

WITH CARLA TOCQUIGNY
My Journey: Travel Experiences
Transformed Travel Journal
Life Lessons from Family Vacations

TRULY
SIGNIFICANT

CONVERSATIONS WITH BIG HEARTED PEOPLE

RICK TOCQUIGNY

WordCrafts Press

Truly Significant
Copyright © 2025
Rick Tocquigny

Hardback ISBN: 978-1-962218-89-4
Paperback ISBN: 978-1-962218-91-7

Cover concept and design by Rick Tocquigny and Mike Parker

Published by WordCrafts Press
Cody, Wyoming 82414
www.wordcrafts.net

TO MY GRANDCHILDREN

Henry and Margot,
it is your future choice to live a life of significance.

Contents

FOREWORD

Rick Tocquigny and I met four years ago on his *Success Made to Last* podcast to talk about my book *Aligning the Dots*. The experience was so positive that we collaborated on several other media projects. Today, I serve as Rick's mentor giving him guidance while he serves others on a variety of boards.

Speaking of serving others, you will enjoy reading 40 stories of people and organizations that serve beyond the call of duty. These 40 "real heroes" don't measure success by the tangible—titles, fortunes, accolades that shine under the bright lights of achievement. As you will read, this tribe's true measure of significance is in the lives they touch, the kindness they extend, and the legacy they leave behind.

Truly Significant is a book that speaks not just to the high achievers of the world but to anyone who has ever wondered: What does it truly mean to make a difference? It is a book of stories—stories of men and women who redefined success not by what they amassed, but by what they gave. Their journeys, varied and vast, reveal a simple but profound truth: significance is within reach for all of us.

This is a book that matters, and here's why.

First, it carries universal relevance. No matter where you come from or what path you walk, the values of kindness, generosity, and meaningful contribution resonate at the core of our shared humanity. These stories remind us that fulfillment is not bound by culture or circumstance but is deeply rooted in the impact we have on others.

Second, it offers transformative insights. Many among us spend years chasing personal ambition, only to find that fulfillment lies elsewhere. The individuals in these pages discovered that selfless giving does not diminish ambition—it elevates it. Their experiences serve as both lesson and inspiration for anyone seeking a greater sense of purpose.

Third, it provides a global perspective. In a world often divided by differences, these stories remind us of the common thread that unites us: the power of generosity to connect, to uplift, and to change lives across borders. Whether in a bustling city or a remote village, the language of significance is one we all understand.

Then, there is hope in action. It is easy to feel small in the face of life's great challenges, to believe that real change is the work of the privileged few. This book dispels that notion. The people within these pages were not born extraordinary; they became extraordinary through the simple yet profound decision to care.

Finally, it invites us to reflect on the legacy of giving. History will not remember the number of possessions we owned, but it will recall the lives we touched. This book encourages us all to redefine success—not as a final destination, but as a journey toward something greater than ourselves.

May you be inspired to live a life of significance.

~Philippe Bouissou, Ph.D.
Managing Director, Blue Dots Partners

Acknowledgments

There are so many people whose thoughts and influence have shaped this book. If you find anything enlightening in this book, it's thanks to the brilliant minds who acted as pioneers in their respective fields doing "works of significance."

A big round of applause and thanks to the team at WordCrafts Press and Mike Parker. Mike has been on this journey with us for the last several years and has ably guided the editorial process and collaborated on the title and book design. Also acknowledging your better half, Paula Parker, for inspiring excellence and standards. Working with the Parkers has been a pleasure.

Heartfelt thanks to Carla, my wife of 45 years. She has been an integral part of every single podcast since 2009 and opined on this book, discussed the order of chapters and gave editorial direction. Most importantly, her unconditional love and support continue to light the way.

I am grateful to my personal mentors, both present and in the past. Some of the special people that molded me were: my Dad and Mom, George and Mary Tocquigny, my Mother in Law, Janell Rohlack, Dr. Lin Yu Tang, Stephen Covey, Coach Dick Swetnam, from P&G: Dan Brooks, Joe Reynolds, Jack Ruppert, Ed Artzt, from Frito-Lay: Vince Gennaro, Al Boulden and Ted Holt, from Publishing: Zig Ziglar, Doug and Emmy Jo Momary, Sue Buchanan, Al Shook, Doug Pilkington, Mark Deuschele, Jim Potts, and Dianne Waggoner, and for life philosophy: First Lady Barbara Bush, Preston Padden, Tim Moore, Dr. Philippe Bouissou, Sallie Burnett, Bill Halamandaris, Sue Lundgren, and Bobby Charles.

And when it comes to lifelong mentors, hats off to my sister Suzanne Key, the most frank person I have ever known.

To my very creative daughters, Heather Tocquigny Barnes and Jennifer Tocquigny, you consistently provide your love and support behind my endeavors.

To their significant others: William Barnes and David Freid. William, you are the Marcus Aurelius of the family. David, you are truly a master storyteller that dances to the beat of your own drum. Thank you for his wisdom on naming this book and for teaching me to find the "story within the story."

To my Grands: Henry and Margot Barnes. You have sparked a new chapter in my life. I hope this book will be a compass for your future life of significance.

Though I am indebted to over 4,000 guests from our *Success Made to Last* podcast, I wish to especially thank our chapter contributors and their stories of significance. I am definitely not the expert. Call me the first recipient of inspiring stories. The real credit goes to Dr. Jane Goodall, Emily Chang, Dr. Ken Blanchard, Dr. Judson Swihart, Dr. Shannon Poach, Pastor Carlos Ortiz, Nina Roesner, Rebecca Nguyen, Mike Berenstain, Viktor Frankl, Dr. Jay Lombard, Cynthia Round, Robin Abb, Margaret Swallow, Sallie and David Burnett, Gary and Ann LeBlanc, Dian Aylan, Pico Iyer, Chanda Bell, Neomosha Nelson, Bill McCartney, Tom Osborne, Sofie Roux, Alice Min Soo Chun, Regina Herzlinger, Jim Henson, Nancy and Johnny Mercer, Dr. Brian Simmons, Dr. Gladys Kalema-Zikusoka, Bob Philipps, General Earl Rudder, Ed Asner, Deb Kielty and The P&G Alumni Foundation.

Special appreciation goes to Team Tocquigny: Dr. Randy Pinto (Physician), Dr. Jim Monk (Dentist), Dr. Jonathan Key (Medical Advisor), Ted Waitkus, ESQ. (Lawyer), Dr. Eric Bryant and Deborah Bryant (Faith leaders), Thomas Hayes (Advisor), Dave

Cooper (Real Estate) Serban Maracine (Financial Advisor), Qing and Monica Mu (Publishing Partners), and Jesus (Truly the Most Significant).

There have been many friends who have been on this journey of significance. You have made a marked difference: Sue and Steve Lundgren, Ken and Rosealie Asarch, Jim and Carol Hartzog, Steve and Allison Feldman, Harlan and Mary Zeinstra, Dr. Jim Monk and Janet Monk, Ed and Nancy Flaherty, Sam and Deb Schreiner, Rolf and Mary Garborg, Keith and Caroline Hurdle, Steve and Mary Roberts, and Clegg and Teresa Williams.

Lifetime friends: Danny Hughes, David Bornowski, Jim and Barbara May, Robin Abb, Bill Sappenfield, Jill Ball, Cheryl Inman, James Wright, Karla Snipes Graham, and classmates from Sherman, Texas, Class of 1974. And from the Class of 1978 at Texas A&M University, these particular Aggies were significant: Paul Mueller, Phil Robinson, Joe Nixon, Glenn Davis and fellow class officers Troby Hoffaker and Gail Hankinson.

All teachers are significant, but these stood out as lifetime muses: Melva Reagan, Barbara Mackey, Mary Ann Dryden, Nonette Kolb, Dorothy Bonsworth, Jewel Perry, Bob Hargesheimer, Brenda Hopper, THE Coach Ed Hunt, Margie Wilson, Bill Wheeler, Bob DeBerry, Paula Morgan, Nancy Jones, Tom Cunningham, Helen Case, Martha Aston, Lan Zeckser along with Principals Tom Kendrick and Tony Fillman.

Significant family members hold a special place in my heart of gratitude: Grandparents John and Lillie Petrick, Papa Alexander Tocquigny, Grandpa Victor Kunz, Uncle Alex and Aunt Marzelle Tocquigny, Aunt Rosalie and Uncle Buddy Oelkers, Aunt Annie and Uncle Joe Gregory, Uncle John and Aunt Gibby Petrick, Uncle Joe and Beverly Tocquigny, Uncle Bobby and LeAnn Tocquigny, Uncle Al and Aunt Margaret Pleshar, Father in law Charlie and Sister in law Nancy Rohlack. I look forward to our eternal reunion.

And remembering my creative brothers that picked up more

skills from our Dad: Dennis and George Tocquigny, Sister in laws; Karen Tocquigny and Terrie Tocquigny.

To our extended family in London: Henrik Kjellin and Georgina Read, in Nashville: Seth and Angela Davis.

Reflecting on Neighbors of Significance, your positive influence mattered: David and Sallie Burnett, Phil and Laurie DesJardins, Tom Bowman, Kathy Dolan and Ron Grayum, Ann and Dave Strand, Brad and Laura Prill, Chris and Annie Collacchi, Karl and Patti Grabowski, Mike and Diane Cwalinski, Tim and Shelli Rolfes, George and Dorene Cleary, Don and Cherie Edens, Scott and Evelyn Brown, Ken and Kathy Koffman, Bob and Catherine Johnson, Sally and Tom Tasker, Larry Telford, Josh Bohn, Joe and Kim McNeeley.

And I appreciate the joy that the Truly Significant Band brings to my life. EV Rodgriguez, Shane Bogardus, Ron Resnick, and Alex Lopez are extraordinary musicians who have come together to create the hottest band in Austin with Latin in their soul. It's an honor to play drums with these friends. Visit www.TSBrocks.com.

And to our future business enterprise friends including Dr. Shannon Poach, Scott and Stephanie Nordhaus, the Ferrara family, Scott Rivello, The Giannis Group, Tanner Rowley and Charlie Pecoraro.

Finally, thank you to more than 4,000 guests on our podcast series *Success Made to Last/Truly Significant* for helping us explore significance, and to all of you who listen.

With appreciation to all for the joyful experience of learning and growing with you.

INTRODUCTION

My mother, a nurse by profession, taught me a simple yet profound truth: If you want to be truly significant, live a life that lifts others up. Her path of caring for the sick and weary shaped lives, one patient at a time. My journey took a different course—one not marked by hospital rooms, but by conversations. Conversations that revealed a tapestry of purpose and meaning far greater than personal achievement.

In 2009, a new frontier was unfolding—podcasting. It was an uncertain medium, a wild, uncharted terrain. Yet, after a handful of interviews, a pattern emerged, a thread that wove its way through every guest, regardless of their background. These individuals had found a joy that transcended material success. Their conversations weren't cluttered with mentions of wealth or possessions. Instead, they centered on purpose, on serving others, on a significance that went beyond the self.

A year later, in 2010, we embarked on a series of 36 interviews with members of the P&G Alumni Network. The result was *When Core Values Are Strategic*, a book that captured the wisdom of some of the most brilliant business minds. And that, as they say, was the turning point.

I still recall speaking with Dian Alyan, a woman who had faced the unimaginable loss of loved ones in a tsunami's wake. Yet, instead of retreating into grief, she founded GiveLight, an organization dedicated to transforming lives. Her story reminded me of a quote by James Keller: "A candle loses nothing by lighting another candle." Each of these remarkable people illuminated lives beyond their own, showing that significance isn't just a personal pursuit—it's a shared light.

And so, we pressed on—another 2,800 interviews. Each conversation added to the growing realization: this work wasn't just about storytelling. It was a journey toward helping people uncover their own purpose. A truth emerged: Our greatest wealth lies not in what we accumulate, but in how we connect.

This book is a collection of stories from truly significant people all interconnected. From Sofie Roux, who at 19, created Bloombox to provide housing for the homeless, all the way to Regina Herzlinger and her husband, working tirelessly to supply life-saving medical equipment to war-torn Ukraine.

Inside each of us, there is a place where purpose resides. It sits alongside kindness and generosity, waiting to be tapped. And when we do, when we embrace the gifts we've been given, we unlock something extraordinary: the ability to live a life of significance.

The truth is, the path to significance is open to each of us. It might start with something as small as volunteering in your own community. And if you're seeking a place to start, there's www.catchafire.org, www.volunteermatch.org, www.engage.org, www.unitedway.org, and www.justserve.org—or visit www.trulysignificant.com.

But in the end, the real story—the one that matters most—begins and ends with you. So as you turn these pages, ask yourself: How do you want to be remembered? Not for your wealth, not for your possessions, but for the lives you've touched. For the difference you've made.

THE FRAMERS

1

SIGNIFICANCE OF MAKING SPARE ROOM IN YOUR HEART

"The meaning of life is to find your gift. The purpose of life is to give it away."

~Pablo Picasso

Emily Chang – Foster Mom, Founder of Social-Legacy

Emily Chang has served in c-suite leadership positions at McCann Workgroup, China, VML, Starbucks China, and for InterContinental Hotel Groups. Earlier in her career she led Retail Marketing for Apple in Asia-Pacific and began her career with eleven years at Procter & Gamble.

Emily is known for her action-oriented, visionary approach, cross cultural team engager, innovative line building, and authentic people leadership.

As an accomplished communicator, Emily has spoken at select conferences and events, including FORTUNE Most Powerful Women Summit and C2 in Montreal, and she has delivered multiple TEDx talks.

With her husband of twenty years, daughter, and rescue mutt, she has spared a room 17 times with young people, five dogs, one turtle, and hundreds of other creatures in God's kingdom.

Visit www.social-legacy.com

Every year, the Chang family gathers around a blank canvas, brushes in hand, ready to paint the vision for their future. And every year, they do something remarkable: they paint over the past. Not to erase it, no—the past remains, forming the foundation upon which new colors, new dreams, new purpose will take shape.

This year, Emily Chang painted a tree. Inspired by John 15, she thought about fruit—good fruit, lasting fruit. But fruit does not simply appear. It requires nourishment, pruning, care. And just as a tree does not grow by accident, neither does a life of significance.

Emily is no stranger to significance. An author, an executive, a mother, a wife—but most of all, a woman who has chosen to make space. Not just in her home, but in her heart. Seventeen children have passed through her spare room, each carrying a story, each seeking a place to belong. And so, Emily did what she has always done: she made space.

The Story of Teo

There have been moments when children—from infants to young adults—have found themselves at the Changs' doorstep, in need of a safe place to live. One such child was Teo, short for Mateo. He was named by the man who found him in poor physical condition.

At just sixteen months old, Teo had endured unimaginable suffering. Born with hydrocephalus, a condition where cerebrospinal fluid accumulates in the brain, his parents had spent their life savings to afford a surgery that could help him. But the so-called doctor they entrusted with their child used nothing more than a household drill to bore a hole into Teo's skull before returning him to his parents. The pain was unbearable. He had lost significant brain tissue and was slowly dying.

Desperate, his parents surrendered him to an orphanage, which, through a chain of connections, reached out to the Changs. Initially hesitant to take on another complex medical case, Emily and her husband deliberated. It was their four-year-old daughter, Laini, who recalibrated their hearts. Overhearing the conversation, she simply stated, "Mom, this is what we do. Of course we're going to take him."

Teo came home with them, and while they thought he might pass within days, his story took a different turn. With multiple surgeries, including a proper shunt placement, he defied the odds. Today, he is eleven years old, a testament to resilience and love. He lived with the Changs on and off for five years, each moment a miracle.

What compels a family to open their doors, to take in the lost, the overlooked? Perhaps it is this: a belief that life is not measured by personal achievement, but by the impact one makes on others. A belief that when we are given gifts—time, talents, resources—we are responsible for using them well. A belief that significance is found not in what we gain, but in what we give away.

This is the essence of social legacy. A lens through which we see both our own unique abilities and the needs that stir our hearts. When these two meet, action follows. For Emily's daughter, Laini, that moment came at fourteen. She saw the divide between how America and China perceived each other—misunderstandings woven into the fabric of media, fear replacing truth.

And instead of standing by, she acted. She created MyShanghai. org, a program to bridge cultures, to reveal the reality behind the headlines. Founded in 2022, MyShanghai is a one-week cultural immersion program for teens and their families that facilitates cultural understanding through an authentic cultural immersion experience. Meticulously curated to provide holistic immersion that exposes participants to Shanghai's fascinating history, rich culture, and local community, Laini leads young people to China, to experience a world beyond stereotypes.

But it does not end there. Significance is not just about vision—it is about leadership. Kenneth Macpherson, the CEO of InterContinental Hotels, understood this. When Emily and her husband took in Teo, a child in need of a forever home, Kenneth did not simply commend her. He acted. Without being asked, he created an adoption policy within the company, easing the financial burden for families like Emily's.

Because leadership—true leadership—is about more than business. It is about people.

Emily learned that lesson well. And so, she lives it. She fosters, she mentors, she writes and does a podcast. She reminds us that we are not called to walk through life with blinders on, focused only on personal success. We are called to look around, to see the need, and to answer it.

And what of you? Perhaps you have space. Perhaps you have time. Perhaps you have a calling you have not yet dared to answer. Emily would tell you to consider this: are you leaving room for what our Creator might have planned? Or are you too busy following your own idea of success?

The world is full of opportunities we cannot imagine. But they are often waiting just outside the plans we have so carefully constructed for ourselves.

And sometimes, the greatest impact begins with a simple act: Making space.

Enjoy our most recent conversation with Emily Chang on Success Made to Last podcast by scanning this QR code.

2

SIGNIFICANCE OF DREAMING BIG
AND SERVING OTHERS

"Servant leadership is love in action. It is about helping others succeed and putting their needs ahead of your own."
~Dr. Ken Blanchard

Dr. Ken Blanchard – Hall of Fame Author, Leadership Guru

Ken Blanchard, Ph.D., continues to have a significant impact on the day to day management of millions of people and companies including our very own Success Made to Last. He is the author of several bestselling books, including the blockbuster international bestseller, *The One Minute Manager ®*, *Leadership and the One Minute Manager*, *Raving Fans*, and *Gung Ho!*

His books have combined sales of more than 18 million copies in more than 25 languages. In 2005, Ken was inducted into Amazon's Hall of Fame as one of the top 25 bestselling authors of all time.

Ken is the cofounder and Chief Spiritual Officer of Blanchard®, an international management training and consulting firm that he and his wife, Margie Blanchard, began in 1979 in San Diego, California. In addition to being a renowned speaker and consultant, Ken is a trustee emeritus of the Board of Trustees at his alma mater, Cornell University.

Learn more at www.blanchard.com.

Dr. Ken Blanchard's life reads like a roadmap for significance, success, and service. From the early days of his career, Blanchard has lived by a fundamental principle: "Associate with people you admire and can learn from." He sought out wisdom from mentors, friends, and colleagues, keeping a notebook to record the lessons he gleaned. This simple act—jotting down insights—became a cornerstone of his methodology and the genesis of his iconic book, *The One Minute Manager*. Three of those insights famously became "One Minute Secrets," compact yet powerful; designed to spark transformation.

Blanchard understands that a good life—like a good business—is built on a foundation of strong, solid values: integrity, love, honesty, and purposeful work. As he wrote in *The Power of Ethical Management*, coauthored with Dr. Norman Vincent Peale, "You don't have to cheat to win." For Blanchard, doing what is right is always more important than being the one who is right. "Humility," he says, "is not thinking less of yourself—it's thinking about yourself less."

Ken's wisdom is underpinned by his belief that "you will be the same person year after year except for the people you meet and the books you read." This philosophy, which he learned from Charlie Tremendous Jones, drives him to forge deep connections and immerse himself in continual learning. He realizes that the path to success is through service. "You can get what you want in life if you help other people get what they want," he says.

Blanchard's career epitomizes the maxim, "Success occurs when opportunity and preparation meet." He meticulously prepares for every endeavor, visualizing desired outcomes, and acting on opportunities as they arise. With his wife, Margie, Blanchard co-founded a 46-year-old global leadership development company. He believes the key to the success of their organization—and any organization—is nurturing its people. "Without them," he says, "you have no company."

Blanchard urges others to dream big but advises, "Never quit your day job until you've got some success under your belt." He distinguishes between hobbies and careers with a pragmatic lens, warning, "If nobody will pay you to do what you love, you have a hobby, not a career." Yet, even as he pushes others to pursue their dreams, he acknowledges the balance required in life. "Becoming a successful entrepreneur and having a spouse are not mutually exclusive," he contends, underscoring the importance of work-life balance.

Blanchard's advice for building a strong marriage is straightforward yet profound: "Spend time together outside of meals and sleeping." He sees marriage as a partnership built on shared values and mutual respect. "You and your spouse are a team," he says, "so act like it."

In business, Blanchard advocates creating environments where people can "soar like eagles." He believes that the most effective approach is to praise people's progress as they work toward their goals. His favorite piece of advice is summed up in a phrase he made famous: "Catch people doing things right!"

Blanchard's belief in the power of legacy helped inspire this book. "We all have legacies," he often reminds his audiences. "Be intentional about making a positive difference with yours." His message is clear: generosity—sharing your treasure, time, talent, and touch—is the path to fulfillment. For Blanchard, giving is far more rewarding than receiving.

Blanchard urges people to focus on what matters most: nurturing relationships, pursuing passions, and contributing to the greater good. "Life is a very special occasion," he says. Don't miss it!"

Dr. Ken Blanchard's legacy is a testament to the enduring power of values-driven leadership. He proves that with humility, perseverance, and a commitment to serving others, anyone can lead a life of significance. "You finally become an adult," he notes, "when you realize that life is about serving rather than being served."

Enjoy our most recent conversation with Dr. Ken Blanchard on Success Made to Last podcast by scanning this QR code.

3

SIGNIFICANCE OF EIGHT LOVE LANGUAGES

"To love and to be loved is to feel the sun from both sides."
~Norwegian Proverb

Judson Swihart, PhD – Counselor and Author

Judson Swihart, Ph.D., is a counselor and well known author of *How Do You Say I Love You?* While he may be retired, he is a force of nature with wisdom and wit. After earning his doctorate from Kansas State University, he practiced at Cornerstone Family Counseling in Manhattan, Kansas.

Judd's focus is on the psychological and emotional roots of love expressions rather than categorizing them into rigid types. He emphasizes that people often struggle in relationships because they assume their way of expressing love is universally understood, when in reality, love must be communicated in a way that resonates with the other person.

It was 1977, and Canoga Park, California, was alive with the hum of industry. Rocketdyne engineers, clad in white coats and thick-rimmed glasses, were hard at work—designing the engines that would one day carry astronauts into the great unknown. The aerospace industry was booming, suburban life was expanding, and with it, a cultural shift was quietly taking place.

But not all frontiers were measured in miles beyond Earth's atmosphere. Some were measured in the distance between two hearts.

Judson J. Swihart was not a rocket scientist, but his work was no less complex. A clinical social worker and counselor, Swihart spent his days in the quiet corners of his office, watching love itself struggle to launch. Husbands and wives sat across from him, frustrated, bewildered—strangers in their own homes. They weren't arguing over money or fidelity, not always. No, their problem was far more elusive. They spoke, but were not heard. They loved, but were not felt.

Swihart saw a pattern. Some husbands worked tirelessly to provide, believing their financial support said "I love you" loud and clear. Some wives poured their energy into acts of service—cooking, cleaning, managing the household—all in the name of love. Others spoke tender words, seeking to heal wounds with affirmations and reassurances. And then there were those who simply longed for time together, a quiet walk or an unhurried conversation over coffee.

What Swihart uncovered was this: love had dialects, eight of them to be precise.

There was Meeting Material Needs, the language of provision, where love was spoken through gifts and financial stability. There was Helping Each Other, where love meant rolling up your sleeves, lending a hand, and shouldering burdens together. Some needed Spending Time Together, where presence—un-rushed and undivided—was the highest form of affection.

There were the needs of the heart. Meeting Emotional Needs

meant listening, empathizing, and being the safe harbor in life's storms. For others, love was best heard through Saying It with Words, the power of affirmation, encouragement, and appreciation.

But love is also physical. Saying It with Touch meant a reassuring hug, a gentle hand on the shoulder, a kiss that spoke volumes without a single syllable.

There was loyalty. Being on the Same Side wasn't about grand gestures—it was about solidarity, standing together, proving that love meant never facing the world alone.

And finally, Bringing Out the Best—where true love wasn't just about making someone feel good, but making them better. The kind of love that challenges, inspires, and lifts a person to their highest self.

Swihart's revelation was simple, yet profound: people were speaking different love languages without realizing it. A husband might say "I love you" by fixing a leaky sink, while his wife longed to hear the words spoken out loud. A wife might express her love by preparing a home-cooked meal, while her husband ached for a warm embrace instead.

And so, with his book *How Do You Say "I Love You"?*, Swihart put love into words—eight of them. He offered couples not just advice, but a map: a way to bridge the divide, to understand and be understood, to love and be loved.

If you talk to Judson Swihart today, he will remind you that three things remain: faith, hope and love. But the most significant is love.

Enjoy our conversation with Dr. Judson J. Swihart on *Success Made to Last* podcast by scanning this QR code.

4

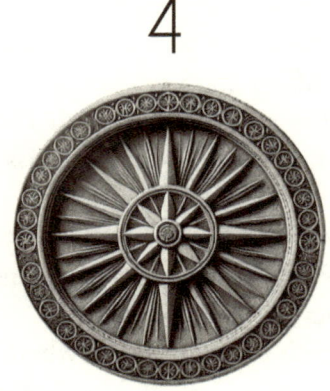

SIGNIFICANCE OF EMOTIONAL INTELLIGENCE

"Emotional intelligence can help you discriminate between feelings and emotions and ultimately guide your thinking and actions."

~Shannon Poach Ph.D.

Dr. Shannon Poach – Psychologist, Co-Founder of The Right One

Shannon L. Poach, Ph.D., is a licensed clinical psychologist based in Torrance, California. He holds a Ph.D. from the California School of Professional Psychology and has been practicing for over 22 years.

For many, coming to therapy can seem like a leap of faith. Psychotherapy asks you to trust a process, and someone, new and unknown to you and to set aside time for yourself in your busy life. Dr. Poach works with individuals experiencing Life stressors including: Bereavement; loss of loved one, pets, and relationships—College Transition; academic pressure, roommate difficulty, independent living—Relationship Difficulties; break-ups, poor communication skills—Family relational issues; blended/step family integration—Graduate School Stressors; organizing schedules, dissertation difficulties, and defining career paths.

In addition to his clinical practice, Dr. Poach co-founded "The Right One" with Scott Nordhaus, aiming to assist singles in finding love through the application of emotional intelligence principles.

Visit www.poachconsulting.com and www.therightone.net.

Shannon Poach was the kind of kid who listened. While the other children raced their bikes down the hills of his small Washington town, Shannon would pause when someone needed to talk. He had an ear for trouble, a heart for understanding, and an uncanny ability to see the emotions beneath a person's words.

It was a gift, though he didn't know it at the time.

Years passed, and that same young boy—who had once sat on his grandmother's porch listening to his neighbors' troubles—grew into a man who made listening his life's work. As a psychologist, he spent decades inside rehabilitation centers, hospitals, and counseling agencies, unraveling the complexities of human emotion. He counseled the brokenhearted, guided the lost, and helped mend fractured relationships. He thought he had seen it all.

And then, he found himself on the other side of the couch.

His own divorce left him adrift in a world he never imagined navigating—modern dating. The apps, the endless swiping, the superficial connections. A world where relationships were reduced to digital chemistry and where loneliness persisted, despite an abundance of options. Shannon saw what was missing.

Emotional intelligence.

He recalled the research of Salovey and Mayer, who had first defined emotional intelligence in 1990 as the ability to monitor and manage one's own emotions while perceiving and responding to the emotions of others. He revisited the groundbreaking work of Drs. John and Julie Gottman, who had spent a lifetime studying what made relationships last. And then it hit him—perhaps the problem wasn't that people couldn't find love.

Perhaps the problem was that people weren't being prepared for it.

And so, he built The Right One along with his best friend Scott Nordhaus.

It wasn't just another dating app. It was a relationship concierge—a movement toward deeper, more meaningful human connection. The Right One wouldn't just introduce you to someone who liked the same music or shared your favorite vacation spots. No, it would match you based on something far more important: your emotional blueprint.

"Perceiving emotions is the foundation of connection," Dr. Poach explains. "It's about recognizing feelings in yourself and others—not just words, but tone, expressions, body language. The Right One helps users identify their own emotional patterns before seeking a partner. Because if you don't understand yourself, how can you expect someone else to?"

But it didn't stop there.

Dr. Poach knew that emotions weren't just felt; they shaped decision-making. "Emotions influence how we approach life's challenges. They can cloud our judgment or make us laser-focused. The Right One takes this into account, ensuring that emotional priorities align between matches. Because a couple's ability to handle conflict together is just as important as their ability to have fun together."

The key, he believed, was not just understanding emotions but managing them. "Many relationships fail not because people don't love each other, but because they don't know how to regulate their emotions in tough moments. The Right One doesn't just pair you with someone who shares your interests. It pairs you with someone who has the emotional capacity to weather the storms with you."

Emotional intelligence was the missing ingredient, the factor that transformed fleeting attraction into lasting partnership. And here's the part that gave Dr. Poach the most hope: emotional intelligence could be learned.

"Unlike IQ, which is largely fixed, emotional intelligence can be developed over time," he says. "That's why we're not just finding you the right person—we're making sure you're ready to be the right person."

To that end, The Right One would go beyond matchmaking. It would equip its users with tools—coaching, assessments, even an emotional intelligence academy—to help them grow into their best selves. Because love isn't just about finding someone.

It's about being someone.

And as loneliness rises in an increasingly digital world, Dr. Poach believes The Right One is more than a solution. It's a revolution.

"We live in an era where people are more connected than ever, yet they feel more alone than ever," he says. "Relationships are the foundation of a meaningful life. And when those relationships suffer, everything else follows. The Right One is here to change that. To not only help you find the right person but to help you build the kind of relationship that lasts."

Listen to the entire conversation with Dr. Shannon Poach on *Success Made to Last* podcast by scanning this QR code.

5

Significance of Radical Candor

"Being truly significant isn't about seeking approval or avoiding discomfort; it's about making a meaningful impact by speaking truth with compassion."

~Life Lessons

Kim Scott – Author of Radical Candor

Kim Scott, is the best selling author of *Radical Candor* and *Radical Respect*.

Kim was a CEO coach at Dropbox, Qualtrics, Twitter, and other tech companies. She was a key member of the faculty at Apple University and before that led AdSense, YouTube, and Double-Click teams at Google.

She learned the most valuable, but painful lessons as co-founder and CEO of two failed start-ups. Kim shares what she has learned from successes and failures alike at the executive education company she co-founded and on her acclaimed management podcast she co-hosts.

Visit: www.radicalcandor.com

A few years ago, a tech executive turned coach walked into a boardroom with the audacious belief that honesty could be kind and kindness could be honest. That woman was Kim Scott. You might know her for shaping the success stories (at the C-Suite level) of Google's AdSense and YouTube, or for mentoring CEOs at Dropbox and Twitter. But what if you learned her greatest contribution wasn't just to business, but to families?

Kim Scott wrote *Radical Candor*, a book about care and candor in the workplace, but what she discovered along the way is that these principles work even better in the home—where honesty and love intersect daily.

Kim defines Radical Candor with two deceptively simple ideas: care personally and challenge directly. In business, this means creating an environment where people bring their whole selves to work. At home, it means raising children who know they are loved enough to hear the truth—and tell the truth back.

Kim explains: "Radical Candor isn't measured by your words—it's measured by how your child hears them. If they're upset, lean into care personally. If they're brushing you off, it's time to challenge directly."

Kim's first lesson in Radical Candor came, not from a corporate boardroom, but her grandmother's kitchen. After catching young Kim in a lie, Grandma Scott told her, "I'm saying this because I love you. If you can learn to be honest and listen when others call you out, life will be better."

That lesson stuck. It became the cornerstone of how Kim raises her own children, blending honesty with empathy. But, oh, it isn't always easy.

Take the never-ending screen time debate. When her kids begged for unlimited access, Kim did something radical—she let them try it for a month. They tracked usage and discovered she was right; self-regulation wasn't happening. Kim didn't say, "I told you so." Instead, she showed them the data and set clear boundaries.

Her children pushed back, as all children do. Kim's response? "When I know I'm right, I stick to the rule. When I'm unsure, I let them experiment and learn for themselves."

One time, her teenage son pushed Kim toward her own therapist's couch. After being asked how she could improve as a parent, he quipped, "Mom, come to therapy with me. How else will you know what you're doing wrong?" Kim laughed and listened—a hallmark of Radical Candor.

Kim has even taken her message to third graders, turning a complex idea into something a classroom of 9-year-olds could grasp. She recounts: "They immediately understood the consequences of being *too nice*—and how to be kind without sugarcoating the truth."

And isn't that what we want for the next generation? Children who grow into adults unafraid to speak honestly, yet tender enough to listen deeply?

Radical Candor at home, Kim says, isn't just about what you say. It's about what you leave unsaid. Small omissions—leftover "feedback debt," she calls it—can erode trust over time. Her advice? Say the hard things, but wrap them in love.

Kim reflects: "Radical Candor has made me a better parent, a better partner, and a better person. Love and truth are not in conflict. To love someone fully, you must be truthful. To be truthful, you must care."

So while the world applauds Kim Scott for her Silicon Valley brilliance, her most profound legacy may be the children she raises and the families her work touches. Because when honesty and love walk hand-in-hand, the result isn't just success—it's significance.

Listen to the entire conversation with Kim in this *Success Made to Last* Podcast by scanning this QR code.

6

SIGNIFICANCE OF A GIVING HEART

"Generosity is truly significant because it transforms not just the receiver, but the giver as well. It creates ripples of kindness, strengthens communities, and leaves a legacy of compassion that outlives us all."
~Jennifer Tocquigny, Many Moons Entertainment

Tomaso Cavasos and her grandson, Carlos Ortiz, Senior Pastor, Gateway Church, Austin, Texas

Tomaso Cavasos, is the beloved grandmother of Executive Pastor Carlos Ortiz at Gateway Church in Austin, Texas. Since he came on staff in January 2020, Carlos has shared the triumphant story of his generous grandmother from the pulpit. She was much more than just a migrant worker. Positively influenced by her core values, unselfishness, generosity, and hard work, you can tell that this good hearted woman made a lasting impact on her children and grandchildren. Her spirit is alive and well at Gateway.

Tomaso would be proud of Carlos as he took the helm of Gateway that has in many ways been countercultural to mainstream Christianity. In a state where polarizing culture can often cause friction around the topic of faith, Gateway Church has found uniqueness in Austin in its anchoring values of "Come As You Are" and "Love Everyone: Life by Life".

Visit www.gatewaychurch.com

In the heart of central Texas, Carlos Ortiz carries the title of Senior Pastor at Gateway Church, a congregation of thousands. But his journey to the pulpit wasn't paved with privilege or ease. It began with examples from his greatest mentors in life, namely his generous grandmother.

You see, Carlos' story is one of legacy—a legacy that began not in the grandeur of megachurch stages but in the humble kitchen of a migrant worker named Tomasa Cavazos, his grandmother. Tomasa, born into the struggles of the fields, found her calling in the simplest of things—corn masa, husks, and a pinch of love.

Life as a migrant worker was grueling. Tomasa, fluent in English, served as a foreman alongside her husband, leading teams of laborers under the scorching sun. But when her family settled in Michigan, her gift for cooking turned into something far greater. It started with foil-wrapped tamales carried to the auto factories by her sons. Soon, the men in the factories wanted a taste, and Tomasa found herself at the helm of a burgeoning side business.

But this wasn't about money.

Tomasa's tamales weren't just sustenance—they were hope wrapped in corn husks. Every dollar she earned was given away, not hoarded. Quietly, without fanfare, she paid tuition for college students, funded mission trips, sent teenagers to camp, and provided room and board for first-generation scholars. When she passed, her pastor revealed a stunning truth: Tomasa, who had never lived a life of financial abundance, was one of the church's most generous givers.

And it didn't stop there. On the Monday before she passed, Tomasa had mailed her tithe. Even after death, her generosity lived on.

Her heart for giving wasn't born out of wealth but out of gratitude. A tent revival in the 1950s had changed her life—and her children's lives—forever. Her faith healed her children when illness struck, and her gratitude fueled her resolve to bless others.

Carlos grew up watching his grandmother's quiet yet significant impact. Her laughter, her stories, and her kitchen became the training ground for his ministry. From her, he learned the power of storytelling, the depth of community, and the joy of unbridled generosity.

Today, as one of the few ethnically diverse senior pastors in Texas, Carlos Ortiz shares his grandmother's legacy with thousands. From the pulpit, he doesn't just preach; he passes down her values. His sermons, like her tamales, are crafted with love and a higher purpose—to nourish the soul and inspire action.

Tomasa Cavazos, a woman of grace, turned tamales into treasure and left a legacy that couldn't fit into a bank account. Her life is a reminder that significance isn't measured by what you keep, but by what you give away.

Enjoy the entire conversation with Carlos on *Success Made to Last* podcast by scanning this QR code.

7

SIGNIFICANCE OF RESPECT

"Respect isn't something you demand. It's something you give—and giving it first is an act of strength, not weakness."
~Nina Roesner

Nina Roesner – Author of The Respect Dare

Nina Roesner has over 25 years in communications and in the training industry, including 15 years with the largest and most significant training company in the world. She has coached numerous executives and pastor in the U.S. and currently provides leadership for Greater Impact Ministries, Inc. as executive director.

She firmly believes that to be fully productive and have significant peace, one must live for the audience of One, being fully engaged in all roles he has placed for us.

Visit www.greaterimpact.org

In 2012, a voice from the heartland emerged—a voice daring us to redefine the rules of respect, not just in our marriages but in our souls. That voice belonged to Nina Roesner, a quiet yet powerful force who penned *The Respect Dare: 40 Days to a Deeper Connection with God and Your Husband*. A book that, like the timeless refrains of Aretha Franklin's "R-E-S-P-E-C-T," struck a chord across living rooms, kitchen tables, and church pews alike.

Now, Nina wasn't trying to write just another marriage manual. What she delivered instead was a guide, a dare if you will, to dive deeper into what makes a relationship not just survive but thrive. And the secret ingredient? It wasn't flowers or chocolates—it was respect. Respect for your spouse. Respect for yourself. Respect as a bridge to something far greater.

But let's back up just a bit. You see, "R-E-S-P-E-C-T" didn't start with Aretha Franklin. The song, as iconic as her voice, was originally written by Otis Redding. His version? A demand for acknowledgment and affection. Aretha's version? A call for dignity and equality. Two sides of the same coin, flipped by the power of perspective.

And Nina? Well, she flipped understanding yet again. Her *Respect Dare* was about something much deeper than just "being polite." It was about recognizing respect as the foundation of significance, as the quiet undercurrent that transforms relationships—not by shouting demands but by walking with grace.

Nina once shared a story about a woman who had spent three decades demanding respect from her husband. Thirty years! And then one day, she realized: "All I had to do was respect him, and he was going to honor me back. I had no idea it was this simple." Simple, yes—but profoundly countercultural.

The challenge Nina posed wasn't just about respect in marriage—it was about redefining respect as an act of humility, strength, and love. And not just in the big moments, but in the tiny, everyday interactions. The coffee poured without grumbling. The calm tone at the end of a long day. The refusal to yell, even when frustration boils over.

She often told her audiences: "Respect isn't something you demand. It's something you give—and giving it first is an act of strength, not weakness."

Of course, not everyone loved this message. Many balked. "Doesn't he have to earn it?" they'd ask. And Nina would point them gently back to scripture, to the grace that we didn't earn but received anyway. Respect, she argued, wasn't about submission—it was about freedom. Freedom from bitterness. Freedom from endless conflict. Freedom to love with Christ-like strength.

And so, Nina's work became more than a book—it became a movement. A movement of women who dared to drink water daily, get enough sleep, and anchor themselves in Scripture before tackling the emotional rollercoasters of life. A movement that understood respect not as a reaction, but as a choice.

And perhaps most importantly, Nina taught us that respect isn't just about how we treat others—it's about how we carry ourselves. "When I lose my temper or yell," she'd say, "I'm not just disrespecting the other person—I'm betraying my own best self."

So as you go about your life of significance, remember this: Respect is more than a word. It's a way of being. And when we dare to live it, we might just find that it transforms not only our relationships but our very souls.

To hear the entire conversation with Nina Roesner on *Success Made to Last* podcast, scan the QR code.

8

Significance of Who You Become

"Even one hair has a shadow."

~Finnish Proverb

Mike Berenstain, son of Stan and Jan,
pens the Berenstain Bears for future generations

Mike Berenstain is an American author and illustrator best known for continuing *The Berenstain Bears* book series, originally created by his parents, Stan and Jan Berenstain. Born in 1951, Mike grew up immersed in the world of children's literature and began contributing to the series in the 1980s. After his father's passing in 2005 and his mother's in 2012, he took full creative control of *The Berenstain Bears*, expanding the series with new stories that often incorporate faith-based themes under the Living Lights imprint.

Before working on *The Berenstain Bears*, Mike illustrated and wrote other children's books, including works on science fiction and fantasy. His artistic style closely follows that of his parents, ensuring continuity in the beloved series. Today, he continues to manage *The Berenstain Bears* brand, keeping the legacy alive for new generations of readers.

Visit www.berenstainbears.com

In the bustling post-war days of the 1940s, two young art students found themselves seated at the same easels in Philadelphia's art school. Stan Berenstain, with a knack for humor and storytelling, and Jan Grant, whose creative genius matched her husband-to-be, formed a partnership that would span decades—and generations.

They didn't know it then, but their life together would be as much about teaching as it was about creating. It wasn't just ink on paper they'd leave behind, but something far more enduring: a set of stories that would teach millions of children—and their parents—what it means to live with purpose, kindness, and love.

Stan had an unexpected detour in his journey before the world ever knew about Brother, Sister, and the whole gang. It was 1941, and like many young men, Stan was eager to serve his country during World War II. But there was one small problem: a childhood accident had left him blind in one eye. This disqualified him from active military service, as the Army had strict requirements for vision, and combat duties weren't in the cards. But the young man, determined not to sit idle while others served, had a different plan—an artistic one.

Instead of putting down his pen and brush, he picked them up and put them to work. The Army, needing skilled artists for something a little less conventional, offered him a role. He wasn't out on the front lines, but Stan's creativity would prove every bit as valuable. He was tasked with creating instructional cartoons, manuals, and safety posters—works that would teach soldiers, keep them informed, and most importantly, keep them safe.

With his knack for humor and simple, yet effective, imagery, Stan's work became an essential part of wartime communication. His cartoons were more than just drawings; they were tools that helped convey complex training materials in ways that were engaging and easy to understand. And though his work wasn't in the heat of battle, it played a vital role in supporting the troops and ensuring they were ready to face the challenges ahead.

35

By the end of the war, Stan had sharpened his craft and had a new purpose. Those same creative skills that helped guide soldiers in wartime would soon give birth to a series that would delight generations of children.

Stan and Jan began a family of their own, and like all parents, they learned as they went—how to guide, how to nurture, how to laugh at the chaos of everyday life. They captured these lessons first in cartoons for *The Saturday Evening Post* and later as creators of a bear family that mirrored their own: *The Berenstain Bears*.

It started with *The Big Honey Hunt* in 1962, a whimsical tale of a bumbling Papa Bear and his loving family. Under the guidance of none other than Dr. Seuss himself, Stan and Jan found a way to make their humor and heart leap off the pages into the minds of children everywhere. But it wasn't just entertainment they were after. They had a higher calling.

Through their books, the Berenstains tackled the very things families wrestle with daily—truth-telling, kindness, sharing, and the importance of pitching in. They knew children learned best through stories that reflected their world, told with humor and love. The Bear family wasn't perfect, and that was the point. Papa made mistakes, Mama showed patience, and Brother and Sister Bear faced the same struggles as every child who ever had to clean their room or stand up to a bully.

What was the real magic of the Berenstains' work? They didn't just tell stories; they taught significance. To treat others as you'd like to be treated. To own up to your mistakes. To find joy in the simple things—a family picnic, a bedtime story, or a bear hug. These weren't just lessons for the Bear family; they were lessons for life.

When their son, Mike, joined the family business in the 1980s, he brought his own perspective to the stories while keeping his parents' values alive. Together, they proved that the core of the Bear family's success wasn't just clever rhymes or charming illustrations. It was the heart behind it all—a belief that families, no matter how imperfect, could be the greatest source of love, learning, and growth.

Even after Stan and Jan passed away, their legacy thrived. *The Berenstain Bears* continued to inspire, proving that the lessons they taught—about kindness, empathy, and doing the right thing—were timeless. In a world that often measures success by status or possessions, the Berenstains dared to suggest something different: that the true measure of a life well-lived is how much we give to others.

And so, through the Bear family's adventures, the Berenstains remind us all of this simple truth: significance isn't found in what we achieve, but in who we become—and how we love.

Enjoy the entire conversation with Mike on *Success Made to Last* podcast by scanning QR code.

9

Significance of Forgiveness

"In choosing to forgive, we uplift both ourselves and others, shaping a legacy of compassion and strength."
~Norman Garcia

Mariana Karama – Pacification Knot

Mariama Kamara was just an ordinary woman, until her son was brutally murdered in Sierra Leone. In one extraordinary moment, she forgave the murderer and adopted him as a family member. To Mariama, forgiveness is of true significance because it freed her heart from the weight of resentment, allowing her to live with grace, wisdom, and purpose again.

Back when we were broadcasting *Mentoring Monday*, I was told a story of forgiveness so profound, it could soften even the hardest of hearts. It begins in a small village in Sierra Leone, a nation torn apart by an 11-year civil war, a conflict so devastating that it scarred not just the land but the souls of its people. Lives were uprooted, families torn asunder, and a deep, abiding pain lingered long after the fighting ceased.

Amid this wreckage lived Mariama Kamara. A mother who, like countless others, had suffered an unspeakable loss. Her son, her pride, her joy, had been taken from her—murdered in cold blood by a young rebel fighter. This was a time when children, some as young as 10, were turned into soldiers. They were armed, manipulated, and made to commit atrocities in the name of war. Mariama's son was just one of thousands of innocent lives lost.

But this story is not about loss. It is about what came next. Mariama, driven by a deep faith and a belief in something greater than vengeance, did something unimaginable. She forgave. More than that, she took the young man who had killed her son into her home. She adopted him. Yes, you heard that right. The woman who had every reason to hate, to seek revenge, chose instead to heal—not just herself, but him as well.

Why? She said it was her faith. She believed that harboring hatred would only perpetuate the violence that had already stolen so much from her and her country. "I wanted to stop the cycle," she said. "If I didn't forgive, who would? And if I didn't forgive, how could I ask God to forgive me?"

Mariama's act of forgiveness became a beacon in Sierra Leone, a country struggling to heal. Her story was one of many that emerged from the Truth and Reconciliation Commission (TRC), a cornerstone of Sierra Leone's post-war recovery process. The TRC was established in 2002 to document the causes and consequences of the war, give survivors a voice, and promote healing through storytelling.

The Nation's Path to Healing

The TRC encouraged victims and perpetrators to come forward, to tell their stories—painful as they were. For some, it was a way to confront their past; for others, it was a step toward atonement. In Mariama's case, it was a testament to the power of grace. The Commission's emphasis was not on punishment but on reconciliation, fostering understanding and dialogue to rebuild trust in a fractured society.

Alongside the TRC, the Special Court for Sierra Leone held accountable those who bore the greatest responsibility for war crimes. This dual approach—retributive justice through the court and restorative justice through the TRC—helped address the country's complex needs. Yet it was stories like Mariama's, rooted in community-based reconciliation, that truly captured the heart of the healing process.

In many villages, traditional rituals were performed to reintegrate former combatants, including child soldiers, back into society. These ceremonies cleansed them of spiritual guilt and symbolized their return to the community. Programs were also established to provide counseling, education, and vocational training, giving these young people a chance to build new lives.

Forgiveness: A Significant Cornerstone of Reconciliation

Forgiveness became more than a personal choice; it became a national movement. Many survivors, inspired by their faith and cultural values, chose to forgive publicly. Not to forget, but to free themselves from the burden of hatred. This collective decision to prioritize forgiveness over vengeance created the foundation for rebuilding trust and community bonds.

But forgiveness is not easy. It's not quick. It's not painless. Mariama admitted there were days when anger threatened to consume her. Yet, she persisted. "When I looked at that boy," she said, "I saw someone else's son. I saw a child who was lost, just like I had lost mine."

Sierra Leone's reconciliation process was not without challenges. Resources were limited, and skepticism ran high. Some felt the TRC's focus on forgiveness let perpetrators off too easily. Others questioned whether traditional rituals could truly heal such deep wounds. But for all its imperfections, the process offered lessons for the world:

- Community Involvement is Key: Healing must happen at the grassroots level, where the wounds are most deeply felt.
- Justice and Forgiveness Must Coexist: While courts address accountability, reconciliation requires the courage to forgive.
- Storytelling is Healing: Sharing and hearing stories fosters empathy and understanding, bridging divides.

Today, Sierra Leone's journey toward peace and reconciliation serves as a beacon for other nations emerging from conflict. It shows that even in the aftermath of unimaginable suffering, forgiveness can light the way forward. And Mariama Kamara? She reminds us all of the profound truth that healing begins not with retribution, but with grace.

Enjoy more of the conversation with Mariama Kamara on *Success Made to Last* podcast by scanning QR code.

THE MOVERS

10

SIGNIFICANCE OF A SENSE OF PURPOSE

"Those who have a 'why' to live, can bear almost any 'how'."
~Dr. Viktor Frankl

Viktor Frankl – Author, Neurologist, Psychiatrist, Holocaust Survivor
with his protege, Bill Halamandaris

Bill Halamandaris' personal mentor was Dr. Viktor Frankl, Holocaust survivor and author of *Man's Search for Meaning*. Viktor shaped Bill's life in the most significant way, turning his heart to a lifetime of service.

Bill is the son of an immigrant coal-miner. For 15 years, he headed a Congressional Committee to find and prosecute waste and fraud. In 1985, disheartened by the corruption he'd uncovered, he began to search for the "heart of America"—people who represent the best in our society, the best instincts of man, and the best part of ourselves. That effort grew into The Heart of America Foundation, a non-partisan non-profit that gives support to groups trying to better our society, especially our children.

Bill is the author of several books including his newest novel—*Blood Runs Deep, The Hill, Spiritual Common Sense: 77 Guiding Principals for a More Meaningful Life, Love & Hate: The Story of Henri Landwirth, His Name is Today: Bob MacAuley and Americares, The Heart of America*, and *Be the Light*.

Visit www.billhalamandaris.com

Viktor Frankl was born in 1905 in Vienna, Austria. He had a childhood marked by curiosity—a boy fascinated with what it means to be human. As a young man, he studied medicine at the University of Vienna under none other than Sigmund Freud. But Viktor? He chose his own road, veering away from Freud's focus on pleasure. Instead, Viktor championed something deeper: the *will to meaning.*

And he would need that sense of purpose… because life would test him in unimaginable ways.

Viktor Frankl was a neurologist, a psychiatrist, a Holocaust survivor, and the father of logotherapy—a belief that finding meaning is what keeps the human spirit alive. When Bill Halamandaris first met him, he expected to meet a giant of a man. But instead, he found Viktor, barely five feet tall, humble, even shy. And yet? He carried a quiet wisdom that could fill a room and transform a life.

During the Holocaust, Viktor Frankl endured unspeakable horrors. He lost his wife. His parents. His siblings. And still, amid the atrocities of Auschwitz, Viktor made an observation that would change the world: those who survived often had something larger than themselves to live for. A dream. A purpose. A loved one.

He would later write, *"Man's Search for Meaning."* That book sold millions, but it wasn't just a story—it was a guide. Viktor showed that even in suffering, meaning can be found. In fact, *it must be found.*

Viktor believed suffering wasn't an enemy but a teacher. He often said, *"The question is not whether we will suffer, but how we will respond when suffering comes."* Pain, Viktor believed, could strip away our illusions and leave behind what really matters: love, purpose, and the courage to live.

Logotherapy—his life's work—taught that life isn't about chasing pleasure or power but answering life's questions. And those questions? They come at us every day. He'd say, *"Man is not the one who asks; he is the one who is asked."*

Even in today's noisy world, with its distractions of technology, instant gratification, and materialism, Viktor's wisdom holds. *Turn off the noise,* he would say. *Seek stillness. Meaning doesn't come to you—you go to it.*

Now, you'd think a man like Viktor might've lost his faith in God after Auschwitz. But no. Viktor believed God was there, even in the camps. Watching. Waiting. Asking, *"How will you respond?"*

And he knew the answer. It was love. Not just feeling love but *acting* on it. Loving others, even when it's hard, even when it's costly. That kind of love, Viktor said, could crack the code of life itself.

In a time of individualism and ego, Viktor left us with a blueprint for significance. He taught us to ask the hard questions, face fear with courage, and find meaning in the darkest places. But most of all? Viktor Frankl reminded us that life's most significant calling is love—an act that enriches the giver and redeems the world.

Enjoy the entire conversation with Bill Halamandaris on *Success Made to Last* podcast by scanning this QR code.

11

Significance of Intersecting Neuroscience, Faith, & Purpose

"Every brain is a universe—where science and faith meet."
~Dr. Jay Lombard

Dr. Jay Lombard – Neurologist and Award-Winning Author

Dr. Jay Lombard is a board-certified neurologist, author, and keynote speaker renowned for his integrative approach to brain health and the treatment of complex neurological disorders. He co-founded Genomind, a biotechnology company focused on personalized medicine for neuropsychiatric conditions, where he served as Chief Scientific Officer and Medical Director.

Throughout his career, Dr. Lombard has held several prominent positions, including Chief of Neurology at Bronx Lebanon Hospital and Westchester Square Medical Center. He also served as a clinical assistant professor at New York Presbyterian Hospital and Albert Einstein College of Medicine.

In 2017, Dr. Lombard authored *The Mind of God: Neuroscience, Faith, and a Search for the Soul*, a book that delves into profound spiritual questions through the lens of neuroscience. Drawing from case studies in his behavioral neurology practice, he explores topics such as the nature of God, the purpose of life, free will, and the concept of the soul.

Visit www.mindfulneuro.com

Dr. Jay Lombard's journey isn't one you hear every day. Neuroscience, faith, and the search for the soul—each element, in its own right, seems daunting, elusive. But for Dr. Lombard, these weren't separate pursuits. They were one.

As a young boy in New York City, Jay Lombard didn't just dream of the stars; he wondered what dreams were made of. What *is* a thought? Why do some moments fill us with purpose, while others leave us searching? For young Lombard, these weren't fleeting curiosities. They were the first whispers of a lifelong calling.

Years later, after earning his medical degree at Nova Southeastern University and completing his residency at Long Island Jewish Medical Center, Lombard began practicing neurology in a world where the brain was studied as a machine. "See a symptom, find the malfunction, fix the wiring," his mentors said. But Lombard had a gnawing question they couldn't answer: What about the *soul?*

In time, he became more than a neurologist. He was a bridge-builder, walking the narrow path between the tangible and the intangible, between medicine and meaning. It was a young patient—a child battling a rare neurological disease—who transformed his career into a mission. "There were no answers I could give his parents to explain his suffering," Lombard shared. "And that's when I began searching for answers no textbook could provide."

The search culminated in *The Mind of God: Neuroscience, Faith, and a Search for the Soul*, a book that challenges the age-old idea that science and spirituality are opposites. With an editor like Gary Jansen at Random House asking, "Can the brain say anything about faith?" Lombard dove deeper than ever. The answers were astonishing.

Faith, he discovered, isn't a coincidence of culture or upbringing. It's woven into the very fabric of our biology. Brain imaging revealed something extraordinary: regions tied to empathy, compassion, and connection lit up when subjects contemplated God, love, or purpose. This wasn't the "God of the gaps," some placeholder for what science hadn't yet explained. No, this was faith as a fundamental part of what it means to be human.

Lombard spoke passionately about the brain's "default mode network," the place where memories, emotions, and meaning collide. "When this network is in harmony," he explained, "we feel whole. But when it's disrupted, as in PTSD or depression, life feels fragmented, without coherence."

And then there was that boy. The autistic teenager who couldn't speak, but who typed profound truths on a letter board. "He taught me that the soul speaks in ways we don't always understand," Lombard said, his voice catching. "It's there. Always. Even when the world is silent."

It's tempting to think of neuroscience as cold, clinical, detached. But for Dr. Lombard, every brain is a universe—a place where science and spirit meet. "The mind is more than a network of neurons firing in unison," he said. "It's where we find meaning, where we connect to something greater than ourselves."

And that something? Lombard doesn't demand you call it God. But he believes that acting as though a higher power exists changes how we live. "Purpose, compassion, and connection—these are the markers of a life lived fully," he said. "Faith isn't an escape from reason; it's the lens through which reason becomes meaningful."

Today, Dr. Jay Lombard continues his work, inviting others to join him in asking the big questions. "We're hardwired for faith," he says, "but we often forget it in the noise of modern life."

And so, from a little boy in New York to a man bridging the worlds of science and soul, Dr. Lombard reminds us of something timeless: That the greatest frontier isn't the stars above us or the oceans around us—it's the mind within us

Enjoy the entire conversation with Dr. Jay Lombard on *Success Made to Last* podcast by scanning this QR code.

12

SPEEDING UP SIGNIFICANCE

"The greatest urgency is not in what we achieve for ourselves, but in how swiftly we move to lift others up. The world needs our help now, not someday."

~Petie Tocquigny

Richard Lackey – Founder of World Food Bank

Richard Lackey, Chairman and CEO of The World Food Bank is featured in this chapter. After leaving a prestigious position in the financial world, his vision is to create a unique model to cure food insecurity. As a for-profit company for one, they have designed a system across multiple connected geographies, typically a country or countries, in order to create a suitably diversified system. The World Food Bank connects farmers with everything needed to build an integrated agricultural system.

By teaching farmers best practices to share with others, and providing access to the tools, marketplace, and the financing—it all creates a sustainable business model for small-hold farmers to find success, relieving poverty, and leading to sustained food availability.

Visit www.worldfoodbank.org and support their foundation at www.wfbfoundation.org

A mother, desperate. A choice no parent should ever face. Typhoon Haiyan had ravaged the Philippines, leaving destruction, hunger, and despair in its wake. There was no food. Not for one day. Not for two. But for twelve long, merciless days. And so, in the face of the unthinkable, she made a decision—one child would live, the other would be left behind.

Richard Lackey watched this unfold on a newscast, and at that moment, something deep inside him broke. A man who had spent his career mastering the art of financial markets, arbitrage, and inefficiencies had just discovered the greatest inefficiency of all—food.

And the question burned within him.

Why can't we save lives within 24 hours of a natural disaster?
Why can't we speed up significance?

So he turned to his wife and said, "God is calling us to do something a little more substantial." And with that, the journey began—from Iowa to Africa, from knowledge to action.

The idea was radical in its simplicity: Buy grain. Employ technology to enable storage for 20 years. Make it investible. Keep food availability constant in regions where scarcity had become the cruel norm. But more than that, teach farmers to grow more. Grow better. Use regenerative practices. Less waste. Less chemicals. More yield. More life.

In Uganda, they met Henry, a farmer with a vision. He understood that regenerative agriculture wasn't just about better crops—it was about community. Farmers learned together, worked together, and grew together. And together, they transformed their future.

But what does this tell us about significance?

That we will never lift two billion people out of poverty alone. That, by divine design, we are called to work in community, holding one another accountable to a higher purpose.

Hunger is not just a problem of the Third World. It exists in the back alleys of New York, in the school lunchrooms of Chicago, in the forgotten rural towns of America. Hunger Action Month reminds us that no one should go hungry. Not when there is enough food in the world to feed everyone. Not when the only thing standing in the way is inefficiency.

And so, Richard Lackey did what he does best—he found a way to eliminate the inefficiency.

Through his work in financial markets, he had seen inefficiencies before. But this? This was the most glaring inefficiency of all. In 2011, a single farmer in Uganda came onto his radar. The collaboration that followed would become the bedrock of the World Food Bank.

Think of it like this: A bank stores money. The World Food Bank stores food. Food with a shelf-life of 20 years. Food that can be distributed quickly, efficiently, strategically—before hunger turns to crisis, before desperation leads to impossible choices.

The World Food Bank is an institutional investment entity, but its currency is human life. It works to ensure that smallholder farmers—who produce over 80% of food in the developing world—can break free from the cycles of volatility that keep them trapped in poverty. It employs the latest in food drying and storage technologies to eliminate waste and ensure stability. It builds networks where relief is not an afterthought but a standing army, ready to respond at a moment's notice.

But Lackey's work did not stop there. His latest initiative, the Zero Hunger Formula, is an interactive, data-driven platform that connects people across the globe with real-time information on agriculture, hunger, and food security. More than a tool—it's a movement, an invitation to collaborate, to innovate, to act.

"We can eliminate hunger," Lackey declares. "Not someday. Not in theory. But now. In our lifetime."

And in doing so, not only can we feed the world, we can also lift its poorest farmers from poverty to middle income, unleashing an economic revolution unlike anything we've seen in history.

The origin story of the World Food Bank is not just about food. It is about hope. It is about faith in a better way. It is about refusing to accept that hunger is inevitable.

More than 800 million people are food insecure. But what if they weren't? What if the key to ending hunger was already in our hands? What if we had, right now, the ability to change everything?

Because we do.

Enjoy the entire conversation with Richard Lackey on *Success Made to Last* podcast by scanning this QR code.

13

HOW A LIFE OF SIGNIFICANCE CHANGES YOU

"The measure of a life is not its duration, but its donation."
~Peter Marshall

Cynthia Round – Former United Way Executive

Cynthia Round is a seasoned brand strategist renowned for revitalizing legacy brands and engaging new audiences. Her career encompasses significant roles at Procter & Gamble, Ogilvy & Mather, United Way Worldwide, and The Metropolitan Museum of Art (The Met).

When Cynthia joined United Way Worldwide as Executive Vice President of Brand Marketing and Strategy, her efforts were instrumental in the organization's fundraising efforts, which amounted to $5 billion across 40 countries.

Beyond her executive roles, Cynthia has been an active speaker on branding and social change, sharing her expertise at various conferences and educational institutions, including Yale, New York University, Columbia, and Oxford.

Cynthia Round does not know it, but she has been a quiet architect of this book. A guiding star. A personal hero.

This is not the first time her story has been told. Different from *When Core Values are Strategic*, it comes with a new twist, a deeper layer, a fresh lens through which to see the mark she has left on the world.

You see, Cynthia is no ordinary strategist, no conventional executive. She is a trailblazer, a woman who redefined the very currency of success—not in dollars raised, but in lives changed. And lives... oh, how she has changed them. Through her pioneering efforts at United Way, her vision for Goals for the Common Good, she worked to reduce dropout rates, build financial stability, improve public health. Not just campaigns. Movements. Not just numbers. People.

Cynthia has always aimed high. She reminds us that even when goals seem out of reach, the act of striving—of pressing forward, of never settling—is where the real magic happens. Her superpower? Uniting communities. Shifting mindsets. Reminding the world that true significance is not in titles or accolades but in the quiet, persistent work of lifting others.

But where did it all begin?

Let's turn back the pages, back to a young Cynthia Round navigating the corridors of Procter & Gamble, sharpening her marketing acumen, mastering the art of brand storytelling. Then, to Ogilvy Worldwide, where she rose to Senior Partner and Executive Group Director. She helmed campaigns for Unilever, AT&T, Kimberly-Clark, Pepperidge Farm—brands that shaped industries. Yet, amidst the high-profile clients and global strategies, something unexpected happened.

She volunteered. Cynthia's heart was stirred.

You see, it often begins this way. A small thing. A simple, *yes.* Cynthia, ever the strategist, had no idea that when she agreed to lead Ogilvy's pro bono work for United Way, she was stepping onto a new path—one not marked by profit margins but by purpose.

The work was different. It didn't sell soap or shampoo. It didn't drive quarterly earnings. It wasn't measured in shareholder returns. It was measured in lives changed. And that, as it turns out, changed Cynthia.

The shift was subtle at first. The questions she asked in meetings took on a new weight. The stories she told around boardroom tables were no longer about market share, but about impact. She saw marketing not just as persuasion, but as connection—a bridge between those who had resources and those who needed them. And once she saw it, she couldn't unsee it.

Then, Evelyn Lauder came calling. A campaign for breast cancer research. The pink ribbon. A Cure in Our Lifetime. The project was deeply personal for Lauder, and soon, it became personal for Cynthia, too. She saw, in vivid color, how the same strategies that built billion-dollar brands could build something far more lasting: hope.

And so, she leapt.

First to United Way Worldwide, where she didn't just rebrand an organization—she reignited a movement. She crafted a vision so compelling, so urgent, that people couldn't help but lean in. She made giving feel less like charity and more like belonging.

Then, The Met. The hallowed halls of art and history. Cynthia saw something there, too: an institution that needed to open its doors wider, to welcome not just the elite but the everyday. Under her guidance, The Metropolitan Museum of Art became The Met—not just a name change, but a mindset shift. Art for everyone flowing into humanity. A museum for the world.

What began as a career in business became a calling in significance. A new kind of wealth, measured not in earnings but in impact. A new kind of influence, not wielded but shared.

What happened to Cynthia? Here's what she learned by opening her life to the notion of significance.

When you start giving without expectation, something profound happens. Your heart expands. You see struggles beyond your own. You listen differently. You feel more deeply.

You grow more grateful. The small inconveniences of daily life shrink in comparison to the real challenges others face. Gratitude, you find, is the best antidote to discontent.

You become stronger. Acts of generosity release oxytocin, dopamine, serotonin—the chemistry of joy. Science confirms what the heart already knows: giving feels good.

You find purpose. A new kind of motivation takes root. The kind that shifts your focus from career ladders to lasting impact.

And you connect. In a world that sometimes feels cold, giving reminds you: we belong to each other.

"How did the shift to significance change you?" I asked.

Her answer was swift. Certain.

"My business career helped corporations build brands. But my personal rewards multiplied when I focused on changing lives. Now, my days are spent thinking about how we can broaden opportunity, increase access to education, health, public services, art, climate justice. I have a clearer sense of what truly matters. A true north."

Yet, it was not always an easy road.

"When I first entered the nonprofit world," she admitted, "many organizations were *allergic* to branding. They believed mission alone should be enough. I had to reframe branding as engagement, as connection. Gone were the massive marketing budgets. Instead, I had to get creative. I recruited a prestigious global ad agency to work pro bono in 17 countries to spread the Live United movement."

She became a different kind of leader. A better mentor. A wiser coach. High expectations remained, but with a new emphasis—on nurturing, on guiding, on helping others find their own voices.

She also discovered a new kind of motivation. Less about pressure, more about potential. Less about expectations, more about opportunity. She called it "positive stress"—the kind that fuels, not drains.

And so, I asked one more question.

Why should other executives follow her lead? Why should more business leaders open their eyes and hearts to the kind of work she chose?

Her answer is simple:

"Each person defines success differently. Some reach their career goals and wonder, 'What's next?' Often, they turn to nonprofit boards. That's valuable, rewarding. But I was compelled to go further—to devote the second half of my career to social change full time.

"Make no mistake: a nonprofit career is not an escape from hard work or pressure. It is not early retirement. You will work hard, often with fewer resources, sometimes with heartbreaking need. But with the right perspective, that need becomes opportunity. Hope. Aspiration. The chance to leave the world better than you found it."

And to those just starting out, she offers this:

"I meet young marketing professionals filled with passion for humanity, for the planet. They are often surprised to learn that they can build a career in marketing while changing the world. My mission now? To recruit as many as possible into this path of significance. No reason to wait until later in your career. We need you now."

Enjoy the entire conversation with Cynthia Round on *Success Made to Last* podcast by scanning this QR code.

14

SIGNIFICANCE OF SERVING SENIORS

One of the deep secrets of life is that all that is really worth doing is what we do for others."

~Lewis Carroll

Robin Abb – The Downsizing Doula, Senior Move Manager

Robin Abb is the Downsizing Doula. Her life and business are dedicated to assisting seniors in navigating the challenges of relocating, downsizing, and decluttering. Robin and her team offer comprehensive services, including sorting, packing, unpacking, and setting up new living spaces. They also facilitate the dispersal of belongings to family and friends, manage estate sales, and handle donations.

Robin's work of significance has earned the reputation as the "competent adult daughter you wished lived close by." Her days are devoted to helping seniors "rightsize" their living arrangements, emphasizing a compassionate and empathetic approach to what can be a stressful process.

Visit www.thedownsizingdoula.com

It was 2024. Years had passed since our serendipitous meeting with lifelong friend, Robin Abb in Niwot, Colorado, where her acclaimed Consignment and Vintage store stood as a sanctuary for those seeking not just treasures, but stories.

Robin had always possessed a unique knack for turning chaos into art, the forgotten into the unforgettable. But in the years since, she'd turned her talents to a new, profound calling—one that would elevate her from a businesswoman to a healer of hearts and homes.

Today, Robin is a Senior Move Manager. But to call her that is like describing Da Vinci as "a painter." It's accurate, yes, but woefully incomplete. In truth, Robin is a Life Therapist, guiding people through some of their most vulnerable and transformative moments.

Her canvas? People's lives.

Her paintbrush? Compassion.

Her masterpiece? Liberation.

In the Olympic Peninsula of Washington State, Robin has become a beacon of hope for hundreds, gracefully blending logistics and empathy into a seamless tapestry of support. Her work goes far beyond the nuts and bolts of moving—it's about renewal, about growth, about helping others turn the page to a new chapter with dignity and purpose.

Consider what a week in Robin's life looks like.

First, the planning. Robin begins by assessing each client's unique situation, crafting a tailored moving plan that feels less like a checklist and more like a warm hug. For seniors facing daunting transitions—downsizing, assisted living, or simply letting go—she brings clarity to the chaos.

Then, the sorting. Ah, the stuff. The decades of stuff. Each item carries a memory, a story, a tear, or a laugh. Robin sits beside her clients as they sift through their belongings, helping them decide what stays and what goes. To them, it feels like untangling the threads of a complicated tapestry. To Robin, it's weaving a new one.

Next, the logistics. Movers, charities, estate sales—she handles it all. Robin's partnerships with Maxsold.com—a virtual estate auction house, and local organizations ensure that each transition is as smooth as it is intentional.

And then, the artistry. Robin doesn't just move people into new spaces; she designs them. She transforms rooms into safer, more functional homes, placing furniture with care, arranging keepsakes with love, and ensuring every corner feels like a fresh start.

But most importantly, the heart work. Robin understands that moving isn't just a logistical challenge—it's an emotional one. For seniors, it means saying goodbye to decades of memories. For families, it means making peace with the past. And Robin, with her signature empathy, is there to hold their hands through every tear and triumph.

While there are hundreds of significant stories to mention, Robin zoned in on Cynthia.

Cynthia was no stranger to pain. She'd lost her son—a grief unimaginable to most. In her darkest days, Robin was there. And through Robin's guidance and encouragement, Cynthia found a way to channel her sorrow into something extraordinary: The Benji Project, a nonprofit dedicated to mental well-being for the youth of Jefferson County.

It started small—a clothing sale organized by Robin that raised $8,000. But today, The Benji Project has blossomed into a movement, teaching teens the life-saving skills of mindfulness and self-compassion. And it all began with Robin's steadfast belief in Cynthia's strength.

So you see, Robin's work isn't just about moving furniture. It's about moving lives forward.

She mediates family conversations about heirlooms and legacy. She creates spaces that are safer for aging bodies and aching hearts. She helps people shed the weight of *stuff* so they can embrace the lightness of possibility.

When it comes to significance, Robin Abb is a living testament to its power. She reminds us that even life's toughest transitions can be moments of beauty. Of liberation. Of hope.

Contribute today to www.benjiproject.org

Enjoy the entire conversation with Robin Abb on *Success Made to Last* podcast by scanning this QR code.

15

SIGNIFICANCE OF REBUILDING DIGNITY

"The only wealth which you will keep forever is the wealth you have given away.

~Marcus Aurelius

Millard and Linda Fuller – Co-Founders of Habitat for Humanity

Millard Fuller was a successful businessman who made his fortune in the field of real estate and business development starting in the 1960's. He co-founded a company called The Fuller Company, which focused on selling and managing property, and he accumulated significant wealth during this time. He became a millionaire by his early 30s, largely through these business ventures.

However, his financial success did not bring him the fulfillment he had hoped for. Fuller became increasingly dissatisfied with the materialism and greed that characterized his life at the time. His growing sense of dissatisfaction led to a spiritual awakening in the late 1960s.

In 1965, Millard and his wife, Linda, decided to turn away from their wealthy lifestyle and focus on serving others. This decision was pivotal in their lives and led to the eventual creation of a truly significant organization known as Habitat for Humanity.

Visit www.habitat.org.

It was the early 1970s, and Millard and Linda Fuller, a young couple from Alabama, had everything they thought they needed. Success? Oh, they had it. Wealth? Piled high. But purpose? That... was missing.

And so, standing at the crossroads of material abundance and spiritual emptiness, they made a radical decision: to give it all away. Not some of it—all of it. Their goal? To start over, not as seekers of fortune, but as builders of something far greater —significance.

Now let me take you to 1976, to the small, sun-soaked town of Americus, Georgia. A couple named Charlie and Lula Mae Moore lived there. Hardworking, humble folks, doing their best to make ends meet. Their home? It wasn't much to speak of—run-down, in disrepair, and beyond their means to fix. They were stuck.

What Charlie and Lula Mae didn't know was that their quiet struggle was about to intersect with the Fullers' newfound calling. You see, Millard Fuller had a vision. It wasn't just about fixing houses—it was about fixing lives. He believed that everyone, no matter their station in life, deserved a decent place to live.

With little more than a heart full of hope and a blueprint for something brand new, the Fullers launched Habitat for Humanity. It wasn't charity. It was partnership.

Enter Charlie and Lula Mae Moore. Their modest dreams, paired with their willingness to help, made them the perfect candidates for the Fullers' experiment. With sweat equity—their hands working alongside volunteers—something extraordinary happened.

Charlie, hammer in hand, and Lula Mae, steady and determined, worked shoulder-to-shoulder with strangers who quickly became friends. Together, they built not just a house, but a home. And in that home? Dignity. Stability. And perhaps most importantly...hope.

But that's not where this story ends. You see, their humble little house became the cornerstone of something far bigger. It was the first of what would become thousands upon thousands of homes, all built on the same radical idea: that when people come together, incredible things happen.

Now, let's fast-forward to 1984. Enter a peanut farmer from Plains, Georgia. You might know him better as President Jimmy Carter. Long after his time in the Oval Office, Carter picked up a hammer—and he never put it down. Alongside his wife, Rosalynn, he helped lift Habitat for Humanity into the national and global spotlight. Over the years, the Carters worked on more than 4,000 homes in 14 countries, inspiring millions to do the same.

But how far did the Fullers' dream reach? Today, more than 46 million people across the globe have found safety, stability, and the dignity of a home through Habitat for Humanity. That's millions of children sleeping soundly under roofs they helped build, millions of parents laying foundations—not just of houses, but of futures.

And what of volunteerism? Habitat did more than build houses—it built a movement. Nearly 1.5 million volunteers annually roll up their sleeves, don their hard hats, and put their hearts into something bigger than themselves.

Here's the point of significance. The Fullers weren't extraordinary people. They were just two souls who said yes—to sacrifice, to service, to something greater. But because they said yes, the world became a little brighter.

So the next time you see a family move into their first home, don't just see bricks and beams. See the Fullers' leap of faith. See President Carter's worn hammer. See the calloused hands of strangers united by the belief that everyone deserves a place to belong.

Enjoy the entire conversation about the Fullers on *Success Made to Last* podcast by scanning this QR code.

16

A CUP OF SIGNIFICANCE

"True greatness consists in being great in little things."
~Charles Simmons

Margaret Swallow – Coffee visionary

Margaret Swallow, P&G Alumnus is a pioneering figure in the coffee industry, renowned for her dedication to empowering women within the sector. In 2003, she co-founded the International Women's Coffee Alliance (IWCA) alongside Karen Cebreros, Colleen Crosby, Kimberly Easson, Karen Gordon, and Melissa Pugash. The IWCA's mission is to empower women across the global coffee community, fostering meaningful and sustainable livelihoods.

Margaret's commitment to women's empowerment in the coffee industry led her to design agricultural and business training to women in Guatemala, Nicaragua, Honduras, Costa Rica, the Dominican Republic 33 chapters worldwide

Her work continues to inspire and empower women globally, fostering a more equitable and sustainable coffee industry.

Visit www.womenincoffee.org

Margaret Swallow devoted 23 years in the corporate world mastering the intricacies of brand management and strategy at P&G with five years working on Folger Coffee brand. She was successful by every conventional measure: a career on an upward trajectory, influence, and a reputation as a trusted leader. But, for Margaret, success wasn't enough.

It was a crisis that became the turning point. A global crisis within the coffee industry revealed a hard truth to Margaret: billions of dollars flowed through an industry that started with small, family-run farms—families that were often overlooked in the economic equation.

For Margaret, this revelation resonated deeply. "It starts with families," she said. "Growing families were part of my essence, whether biological or the family I became part of through life. That, for me, became my coffee family."

Margaret left the corporate world to answer a louder calling: to create significance through the very industry that had captured her heart. She joined the Coffee Quality Institute (CQI), leveraging her skills to help families around the globe. Margaret's efforts were far-reaching, but they started small—with a ripple.

Margaret, who had developed training programs at P&G, saw an opportunity to bring that experience to the nonprofit world. She designed a Women in Coffee Leadership Program, modeled after the Marketing Director College she had once spearheaded. But this program wasn't just about theory; it was interactive, practical, and transformative. From 2005 to 2006, Margaret's program took root, inspiring the creation of the International Women's Coffee Alliance (IWCA).

The IWCA's ripple began as a single chapter in Costa Rica. But Margaret, inspired by the Rotary Club's model of local chapters, envisioned something far bigger. Today, there are over thirty IWCA chapters worldwide, each empowering women in coffee-growing communities to receive funding directly—without intermediaries. "It's about families helping families," Margaret said. "And it's about enabling local leaders to take charge of their own futures."

The ripple effects didn't stop there. Margaret worked with the University of Maryland to establish an alternative break program. Starting in 2010, students traveled to Los Andes, a coffee farm in Guatemala, to experience the harvest firsthand. Over a decade, hundreds of students learned not just about coffee but about the lives and resilience of the families who cultivate it. "I wanted to connect people to a place I'd send my own family," Margaret reflected. And she did just that.

For Margaret, it wasn't just about building programs; it was about fostering relationships. One of those relationships was with Phyllis Johnson, who co-founded the Coffee Coalition for Racial Equity, further expanding the industry's impact and inclusivity. Margaret's work inspired others to create ripples of their own, each wave building on the last.

When asked if she would have followed this path without the crisis, Margaret's answer was measured. "I think so. But the crisis crystallized the need. It made me ask, 'Where can I make the greatest difference?'"

And Margaret's blueprint for creating significance? Start with understanding the need, she advises. Commit realistically and execute with excellence. Whether it's a small epiphany—a "little e"—or a life-altering one, she emphasizes the importance of starting where you can and growing from there.

Would she do it all again? Margaret smiled. "I wouldn't change a thing. Those 23 years at P&G prepared me for this work. They gave me the tools, the confidence, and the perspective. Everything I've done since then has been about giving back, about creating a ripple effect that matters."

The rest of her life is still unfolding, one ripple at a time. Margaret Swallow—a woman who traded success for significance—is proof that the best part of waking up is finding meaning in your cup.

Enjoy the entire conversation with Margaret Swallow on *Success Made to Last* podcast by scanning this QR code.

17

A Place of Significance

Be generous and willing to share time, resources, or support without expecting anything in return. And extend grace to others when they fall short.

~Church Kitchen Ladies

St. Paul Lutheran Church – Taylor, Texas

St. Paul Lutheran Church is a center of faith in Taylor, Texas. St. Paul represents over 300,000 churches across America that serve others with food, fellowship and a lot of grace. We encourage you to discover centers of faith with big hearted people in your community. Thank you to every church volunteer for making a significant difference.

Visit www.stpaultaylor.com

My mom once said that it's easier to enter a church kitchen door than the church door itself. There is truth in that observation when you consider the hospitality at 300,000 church kitchens across America and the 20 million volunteers at work. Their mission? To serve others without any thanks in return.

There is one truly significant church kitchen in the heart of Texas, located in Taylor, northeast of Austin. It is the home of friendly folks, world-famous barbeque, the Taylor Ducks, and St. Paul Lutheran. This is the hub for big hearted people, keeping a small-town spirit alive in the midst of Taylor becoming a semi-conductor chip capital, thanks to the arrival of Samsung.

But technology aside, we're interested in a different kind of power. The power of a kitchen. The power of service. The power of people behind it.

We step through the kitchen door at St. Paul Lutheran to visit where generations have gathered, including my wife, Carla, her mom, Janell, and her grandmother, Norma. We return to Carla's roots to see what's cooking—literally and spiritually.

There is Jeanie Schneider, a veteran church kitchen lady, famous for her casseroles and cookies. You might even recognize her—her caricature graces *Gracefully Yours* greeting cards, celebrating the unsung, humorous heroes of the church kitchen.

On the Saturday night before a potluck brunch, Jeanie shared her secrets. In her home, a handful of faithful friends gathered to talk about St. Paul, potluck traditions, and, of course, pie. There was laughter, wisdom, and a serious commitment to making sure Sunday morning would be just right.

The headline that night? "We are ready to serve whoever walks through the door."

Sunday morning arrives. The Servin' Up team is already in action, led by Rita Kelm. She has volunteered in the kitchen since the very first Sunday brunch. Since 7:45 a.m., Rita, Jeanie, Janet Brinkmeyer, Gayle Collins, Shirley Evans, Wandeen Sankewitz, Marilyn

Artieschoufsky, Carmen McCleery, and Sandra Umiker have been heating up the kitchen, brewing Folgers coffee, sweetening iced tea, and making lemonade. The tables are set for autumn, even though the Texas sun insists it's still summer.

In the narthex, we find Don Artieschoufsky. He has a story to tell. Servin' Up isn't just about food. It's about action. Habitat for Humanity has found a strong ally in St. Paul Lutheran, as has Shepherd's Heart. Through their efforts, they give others faith and resources to help them sustain their lives. They give them a reason to believe, to have the faith they are going to need to press on, and perhaps even help others—paying it forward.

Pastor Qualley welcomes everyone, including those who might otherwise feel unwelcome. The homeless are not turned away. They are not shunned. They are, instead, seen, heard, and fed—both in body and spirit. Because, after all, the words of Christ remind us, "Whatever you did for the least of these, you did for me."

Back in the fellowship hall, the feast is ready. What's on the table today? Burritos. Cheese queso, a recipe from Naomi Pasemann. Chick-fil-A nuggets, Golden Chick, casseroles from—well, almost everyone. And lasagna, because you can never go wrong with lasagna. And of course, a disproportionate amount of dessert. Apple pie from H-E-B—a church kitchen shortcut that still gets the job done. And a peach cobbler from Janell, age 92, who has been serving up sweetness since 1945. Jeanie's cookies are standouts.

We see Christine Rohlack, the first woman president of the congregation. She believes in leading by serving. Her two sons are already following in her footsteps, learning the St. Paul tradition of putting others first. Teaching the significance of service to the next generation is a priority.

And in walks Pastor Qualley into the kitchen, a man with a particular weakness for a church kitchen classic—pimento cheese sandwiches. The plates are full. The hearts, even fuller. This is what a place of significance is all about. Feeding others, and in turn, feeding the soul.

But the real work? That begins on Monday. Because a place of significance isn't just for Sunday events. It's a way of life. It's the home of the Ruth Circle, which serves grieving families, arranging for celebration-of-life meals following funerals. Then there is the next Habitat for Humanity project, filling the pantry at Shepherd's Heart food pantry, the church garage sale, and the opening day for the St. Paul Child Development Center.

As the hymn goes, *His compassion bids us bear, stirring us to ardent service, your abundant life to share.*

It's about bringing what you can in time, talent, and treasure, so someone else can have what they need. It's the heartbeat of a community, and ultimately, a way to serve the Creator who made us all.

What's a place of significance? Anywhere volunteers stand ready to serve others.

Enjoy hearing more about St. Paul Lutheran on *Success Made to Last* podcast by scanning this QR code.

18

SIGNIFICANCE OF TOUCHING LIVES
WITH LITERATURE

"What counts in life is not the mere fact that we have lived. It is what difference we have made to the lives of others that will determine the significance of the life we lead."
~Nelson Mandela

Honoring Andrew Carnegie, Dolly Parton, and Jeff Bezos

A truly significant philanthropist of the past is honored in this chapter, along with with two other individuals that you know well.

Andrew Carnegie, was born into poverty in Dunfermline, Scotland, arriving in America with his family, carrying little more than hope. He works in a cotton mill at the age of 13, earning a mere $1.20 a week. But he reads. He learns. He dreams.

He worked his way to become an industrialist and philanthropist who led the expansion of the American steel industry in the late 19th century, making him one of the richest men of his time. After amassing his fortune, he devoted the latter part of his life to philanthropy, believing in the "Gospel of Wealth"—the idea that the wealthy have a moral obligation to give back to society.

Carnegie is best known for funding the construction of over 2,500 public libraries worldwide.

Visit: www.carnegie.org

Three individuals from different eras and with vastly different means shared a common vision—to ignite the power of words, the beauty of stories, and the timelessness of books for the benefit of humankind. Their names: Andrew Carnegie, Dolly Parton, and Jeff Bezos.

It began with Andrew Carnegie, a Scottish immigrant who came to America with nothing but a dream and determination. Rising to unimaginable wealth during the Industrial Revolution, he saw his success not as an end but as a responsibility. In the late 19th century, Carnegie embarked on an audacious mission: to provide communities with the tools to educate themselves.

The Carnegie libraries—1,689 in the United States alone—were more than just brick-and-mortar buildings; they were cathedrals of learning. From small towns to bustling cities, these libraries opened the door for millions to enter the world of literature, learning, and opportunity. Carnegie didn't just donate books; he planted seeds of hope. He believed, as he once said, that "the man who dies rich dies disgraced." Instead, he died having enriched the world.

Decades later, a voice with a twang as sweet as her home state of Tennessee would carry on this legacy in her own way. Dolly Parton—a country music legend—never forgot her roots in Sevier County. She remembered the poverty, the isolation, and the hunger for more than just food.

In 1995, Dolly founded the Imagination Library, a simple yet profound idea: to deliver free books to children, no matter their family's circumstances.

Today, Dolly's Imagination Library has gifted over 200 million books to children in the U.S. and beyond. From board books to bedtime stories, these treasures have sparked countless imaginations. "If you can read," Dolly said, "you can dream. And if you can dream, you can do anything." Her melodies of compassion harmonized with her mission to ensure no child would ever be without a story to call their own.

And then came Jeff Bezos, a visionary of the digital age. In 1994, he launched a modest online bookstore from a garage in Seattle, naming it after the mighty Amazon River. What began as a humble effort to sell books grew into the largest marketplace in human history. Yet at its core, Amazon's foundation was story-telling—making books, both new and used, accessible to anyone with an internet connection.

Through Amazon, the dusty corners of secondhand shops met the sleek shelves of bestsellers. Independent authors found a global stage, and readers found stories they didn't know they needed. Bezos once said, "We're not in the business of selling things. We're in the business of enabling dreams." And he did. With billions of books delivered worldwide, Amazon has become a lifeline for readers and writers alike.

Three lives. Three visions. One profound impact. Together, these stewards of literacy have helped to ensure that readership is not only up but thriving. Illiteracy is on the decline, and storytelling continues to inspire the next generation.

Carnegie lit the first flame of access. Dolly carried the torch to young hearts. Bezos propelled it into the digital era. The result? A world where books remain the bridge to understanding, empathy, and significant connection.

Enjoy our podcast that honors this threesome on *Success Made to Last* by scanning this QR code.

19

SIGNIFICANCE OF LIVING FOR A GREATER GOOD

"It is up to us to give back to society. It is what makes us great."
~David Burnett

David Burnett – Citizen, Activist, Visionary

David Burnett was a beloved mentor and significant neighbor, known for his deep commitment to community service and philanthropy. He served on the boards of several nonprofit organizations, including the Association for Community Living in Boulder County, EPIC, the Saint Joseph Hospital Foundation, and the YMCA of Northern Colorado. His efforts were instrumental in expanding employer-sponsored childcare and advocating for free universal preschool, reflecting his dedication to enhancing community well-being.

Professionally, David worked as a bank executive with Wells Fargo. He passed away at the age of 55 on July 22, 2022, after a courageous 19-month battle with metastatic colon cancer. His legacy continues through the David Burnett Childcare Center at the YMCA of Northern Colorado, a testament to his vision for accessible early childhood education.

We were visiting the George Herbert Walker Bush Presidential Library in College Station, Texas with David and Sallie Burnett in April of 2022. David took the seat behind the Resolute Desk and said these prophetic words—"It is up to us to give back to society. It is what makes us great."

Not all giants stand tall. Some walk among us quietly, leaving footprints not in sand but in the hearts of those they meet. Such was David Burnett.

Lafayette, Colorado, is like many small towns—a place where neighbors know each other's names, where the rhythm of life hums along at a steady, familiar pace. But every so often, a soul comes along who doesn't just live in a town, across a cul-de-sac, but weaves himself into its very fabric.

David Burnett was that kind of man.

He was more than just a neighbor—he was a force for good. A board member on countless nonprofit organizations, he didn't just believe in making a difference; he did it, over and over again. And not by standing on soapboxes, not with grand speeches, but with something far more powerful: a giving heart, a generous spirit, and the courage to ask others to join him.

Consider this: David served on the board of the Association for Community Living in Boulder County, advocating for those with developmental disabilities. He sat on the finance committee, ensuring funds were wisely allocated to provide services and opportunities for those who needed them most.

At EPIC, he was a trusted advisor, working to expand employer-sponsored childcare. He understood that when working parents had reliable childcare, families and businesses thrived. He worked, not for accolades, not for recognition, but because it was the right thing to do.

He lent his expertise and heart to the Saint Joseph Hospital Foundation Board, knowing that quality healthcare should never be a privilege—it should be a promise.

And the YMCA of Northern Colorado? David's fingerprints are there too. The recent opening of the Inspire Preschool and Infant Care was a testament to his unwavering belief that all children—regardless of background—deserved a strong start. His dream was free universal preschool, a vision he pursued with the same fire that fueled his every endeavor.

Some people shy away from asking for help. Not David. He knew the secret—people want to give; they just need someone to show them how. And he was that someone. A phone call, a handshake, a moment of eye contact—David had a way of making you believe that yes, you could do more, you should do more. And because he believed it, you believed it too.

He and his wife, Sallie, raised their daughter, Brittany, with the same values. She watched, she learned, she followed in his footsteps. Devoting her life to nonprofits wasn't just a career choice; it was a calling, a legacy. Her father's legacy.

And that legacy lives on. Recently, the David Burnett Childcare Center opened at the YMCA of Northern Colorado. Brittany said, "Dad worked so incredibly hard for this project and for free universal preschool for children of all ages across Colorado. His vision was to open access for early childhood education to give them a chance to succeed at an early age. I am proud of his legacy and heart for others."

As for David's career? He was a bank executive with Wells Fargo who happened to see beyond the money and into the currency of life itself.

But even the strongest among us are not invincible. Colon cancer came for David at 55. Too soon. Far too soon.

Yet, some legacies are not measured in years but in lives touched. In lessons taught. In communities made stronger, charities made richer, hearts made fuller.

David Burnett was better than a friend. Better than a brother. More than next of kin.

He was a resolute role model.

Enjoy our podcast that honors David's career on *Success Made to Last* by scanning this QR code.

20

SIGNIFICANCE OF VISION TO HELP OTHERS

"The fragrance of flowers spreads only in the direction of the wind. But the goodness of a person spreads in all directions."
~Chanakya

Dean Butler – Founder of Lenscrafters

Dean Butler is a truly significant figure in the optical retail industry, best known for founding LensCrafters in 1983. Prior to this, he spent 14 years as an advertising executive at Procter & Gamble, where he honed his marketing expertise.

Under Butler's leadership, LensCrafters revolutionized eyewear retailing with the introduction of the "glasses in an hour" concept, significantly enhancing customer convenience and transforming industry standards. The company became truly significant with their creation of One Sight, their flagship philanthropic program changing eyesight to the needy around the globe.

Visit www.lenscrafters.com/onesight

D ean Butler began his journey at Procter & Gamble in 1969. They taught him the fundamentals of success—the art of marketing, the science of sales. But somewhere along the way, something else took hold. A conviction. A purpose. Something that would lead him to put resources not just behind selling products, but behind changing lives.

Dean wanted something more. Something that mattered.

That something came when he founded LensCrafters.

At the time, the optical industry was sluggish. Eyewear took days—sometimes weeks—to be made. But Dean Butler saw a different way, an audacious way. What if glasses could be delivered in an hour?

It was a simple solution. It was a provocative idea. And it worked. LensCrafters revolutionized the industry. No longer did people have to wait. No longer did they have to squint through blurry vision while their lenses were crafted in some far-off lab. It was a game-changer.

But Dean Butler's journey didn't end with just changing an industry. No, he and his team began asking a bigger question: "What other needs can we address?"

Enter *OneSight* and *Gift of Sight*.

Dean had learned from Texas State Optical, one of the first optical chains, and now, LensCrafters had the speed, the infrastructure, and the vision—pun intended—to do more.

My mother, Petie Tocquigny, a school nurse in Sherman, Texas, was part of a nationwide grassroots system that checked children's vision. And now, LensCrafters' ability to deliver eyewear within an hour became a crucial piece of that ecosystem. Children who failed their eye exams didn't have to wait weeks to see the blackboard again. They could get their glasses the same day. A problem solved. A life changed.

But then—then something truly remarkable happened.

In 1985, Delta Airlines Flight 191 crashed at Dallas/Fort Worth

International Airport. Many of the surviving passengers had lost their glasses in the chaos. The airline turned to LensCrafters. And in the very same day, LensCrafters replaced every pair of glasses that had been lost. Vision restored in more ways than one.

And so it continued.

With *OneSight*, a non-profit organization founded in 1988 that has targeted aid to over 330 million people worldwide who suffer from poor vision because they lack the means and access to eye care. LensCrafters and its team set up vision clinics in underserved areas around the world. Free eye exams. Free prescription glasses. Entire communities given the gift of sight.

With *Gift of Sight*, in-store donations and volunteer efforts ensured that children and families who could not afford glasses received them anyway. A basic human need—one that so many of us take for granted—was met with generosity and speed.

And if you're wondering what difference a single pair of glasses can make, let me tell you about María Rodríguez.

María, a 62-year-old grandmother from a rural village in Guatemala, had resigned herself to blindness. Cataracts had stolen her sight, her independence. She could no longer care for her grandchildren, weave the textiles that sustained her family, or even walk safely through her home.

Then, *Gift of Sight* came to her village. She was identified as a candidate for cataract surgery. A simple 20-minute procedure. And the next day, when the bandages were removed, María wept with joy. She could see.

She could see her daughter's face. She could weave again. She could care for her family.

Or consider Rajesh Kumar, a tailor from Uttar Pradesh, India. His world had gone dark, and with it, his ability to provide for his family. But after a free cataract surgery through *Gift of Sight*, Rajesh returned to his sewing machine, his livelihood restored. His first words? "I can work again! I can provide for my family!"

Or Elena Martínez from Oaxaca, Mexico. A street vendor whose failing vision nearly cost her everything. But after her surgery, the first thing she said was, "I can see the colors again!" And with that, she returned to the market, her confidence, her dignity, her life renewed.

For Dean Butler, his true legacy—his *true* significance—was not in what he sold, but in what he gave back.

Because in the end, it's not about the businesses we build. It's about the lives we touch.

Enjoy our conversation with Dean Butler by scanning the QR code.

21

SIGNIFICANCE OF FIRST RESPONDERS

*"Not all of us can do great things. But we can do small things
with great love."*

~Mother Teresa

Mercy Chefs – Encouragement at Natural Disasters

Gary and Ann LeBlanc are the founders of Mercy Chefs, a nonprofit organization dedicated to providing high-quality, chef-prepared meals to individuals affected by disasters and food insecurity.

Their journey began in 2006, following the devastation of Hurricane Katrina in Gary's hometown of New Orleans. Gary, deeply moved by the destruction and the inadequate food relief efforts, felt compelled to act. This led to the establishment of Mercy Chefs, with the mission to deliver restaurant-quality meals during times of greatest need.

Visit www.mercychefs.org

When disaster strikes, the world watches. Homes crumble. Lives are uprooted. Despair settles in like an unwelcome guest. But amid the wreckage, there is a sound—not of the wind, not of the waves, but of hope arriving. A distant rumble. The heartbeat of Mercy Chefs.

You see, Mercy Chefs isn't just a name. It's a mission. A promise. A beacon of light in the darkest of times.

It began in 2006, in the wake of Hurricane Katrina. Gary LeBlanc, a chef by trade, saw something that broke his heart. People—good people—left with nothing. Hungry. Helpless. Forgotten. He knew he had to do something. And so, with a chef's heart and a servant's hands, he set out to change the way disaster relief was done. Not with mass-produced, lifeless rations, but with real food—hot, hearty, and made with love. A meal that could do more than fill a stomach. A meal that could heal a soul.

Since then, Mercy Chefs has served over 28 million meals. But this is not just about numbers. It's about people. Mothers who didn't know how they would feed their children. First responders running on empty. Families holding onto hope by a thread.

But Gary was not alone in this vision. Ann LeBlanc, co-founder and force of nature, saw another need. Hunger isn't just a crisis in the aftermath of storms—it's a daily battle for millions. And so, Mercy Chefs grew beyond disaster zones. They built permanent Community Kitchens, places where dignity is served alongside every plate. First in Portsmouth, Virginia, then in Nashville, Tennessee. Then Dallas. Richmond. And soon, many more.

Now, Mercy Chefs is on the front lines of every kind of devastation—hurricanes, tornadoes, wildfires, floods. But listen closely, and you'll hear the real story. They don't just cook. They connect. They don't just serve. They soothe. They don't ask, *What's in it for us?* They ask, *What can we do for you?*

Because to Mercy Chefs, food is more than nourishment—it's a message: *You matter.*

Their values? Simple. Dignity—because every plate should look as good as it tastes. Compassion—because love, not obligation, fuels their work. Service—because giving isn't a duty; it's a way of life.

They give not what is left over—but their very best. They serve strangers like family. They show up, every time, no matter the cost. Because to them, serving isn't something they do. It's who they are.

But every hero faces challenges. For Mercy Chefs, the hurdles are great. Supply chains fail. Roads close. Food costs rise. The emotional weight of walking into devastation, again and again, is unimaginable. And yet… they press on. Every storm. Every heartache. Every soul in need.

And now you know why. Because to them, serving is living. Their story isn't just about feeding the hungry. It's about purpose. About perseverance. About a love so big it moves mountains, crosses oceans, and stands firm in the face of every storm.

Mercy Chefs. A name you may not hear on every headline. But to the millions they've served? They are the significant difference.

Open your heart and visit www.mercychefs.com today.

Enjoy our tribute to Mercy Chefs on *Success Made to Last* podcast by clicking on this QR code.

22

SIGNIFICANCE OF RESPONDING TO A HIGHER CALLING

"Your greatness is not what you have; it's what you give."
~Alice Hocker

Dian Alyan – Founder, GiveLight Foundation

Dian Alyan is the founder and CEO of the GiveLight Foundation, an organization dedicated to providing loving homes and quality education to orphans worldwide. Born in Takengon, Aceh, Indonesia, Dian pursued a successful career as a chemical engineer and executive at Procter & Gamble. Her life took a profound turn following the devastating 2004 Indian Ocean tsunami, which claimed the lives of 40 of her relatives.

Since then, GiveLight has expanded its reach, building and supporting homes in countries including Pakistan, Bangladesh, Cambodia, Sri Lanka, and Morocco, and sponsoring orphans in regions such as Somalia, Haiti, Afghanistan, Nepal, and Turkey.

Under her leadership, GiveLight has grown into a global institution, positively impacting the lives of over 1,000 orphans across more than 11 countries.

Visit www.givelight.org

Tragedy has a way of reshaping lives, often in the most unexpected moments. Dian Alyan's life took an unforeseen turn on that fateful day, December 26th, 2004. It was a day that forever altered the trajectory of her existence. On that day, her home country was hit by an earthquake of immense magnitude, a seismic force measuring 9.1 on the Richter scale. The ensuing devastation was heart-wrenching, with over 200,000 lives lost in its merciless grip.

Dian hailed from Aceh, a place where dreams of a prosperous life, education, and a loving family were shared aspirations among many. Growing up in central Indonesia, she was immersed in a culture steeped in deep religious devotion and a strong commitment to helping others. Dian's family had a long lineage of coffee farmers, and the values they instilled in her resonated deeply. They taught her the essence of her faith, emphasizing the importance of ethical reciprocity, often referred to as the golden rule: treating others as we wish to be treated.

But it is in the darkest moments of despair and anguish that these principles etched in our hearts ignite with an unparalleled fervor. For Dian, this pivotal awakening occurred during that final week of 2004. The Sumatra-Andaman earthquake, originating off the northwest coast of Sumatra, unleashed a wave of destruction that decimated not only the physical landscape but also the very core of Dian's being. She bore witness to the loss of her loved ones, the annihilation of her homeland, and the profound devastation that enveloped her community. In the face of such utter devastation, she found within herself an unwavering determination to take action.

From the crucible of her resolve emerged Project Noordeen, an initiative born out of a deep-seated desire to help rebuild Aceh, the ravaged Indonesian territory that held her heart. But Dian's vision extended far beyond the borders of her homeland. It was a spark, an audacious idea that would eventually ignite a transformation in the lives of orphaned children around the world.

Dian had traversed the journey of an ordinary child, experiencing the joys of motherhood and achieving success as an executive at Procter & Gamble. Yet beneath the veneer of accomplishment, a persistent yearning tugged at her soul—a desire to create a legacy that transcended personal achievements, to make a difference that would ripple across generations.

It was in the tender embrace of her own child, juxtaposed with the heart-wrenching images of countless children left without parents, that Dian's path took an irreversible turn. Out of the wreckage of tragedy, The GiveLight Foundation emerged, birthing an orphanage that provided shelter and education to fifty children. The name "Noordeen," a tribute to her revered great-grandfather, symbolized the spirit of a man who had fought for Indonesia's freedom from Dutch colonization in the 1930s.

In Dian's own words, she reminds us that the potential to affect significant change resides within us all. Success and philanthropic foundations need not be prerequisites for making a difference. She implores us to start small, within our own communities, to volunteer our time, donate to causes close to our hearts, and embrace the power of every small action. It is through these collective efforts that we sow seeds that grow into a lasting legacy, nurturing generations to come.

Dian urges us to examine the very essence of our lives, to reevaluate our pursuit of purpose. As a culture, we often fixate on our individual destinies, but what about the pursuit of love, of being loved, and of ceaselessly assisting others? This is the revelation that propelled Dian.

Enjoy the entire conversation with Dian A_yan on *Success Made to Last* podcast by scanning this QR code:

THE SHAPERS

23

SIGNIFICANCE OF TRANSFORMATIVE TRAVEL

"We travel, initially, to lose ourselves; and we travel, next, to find ourselves."

~Pico Iyer

Pico Iyer – Travel Writer, Philosopher, Global Soul

Pico Iyer is one of the most renowned travel writers of our time, known for his deeply reflective and philosophical approach to travel. Born in 1957 in England to Indian parents, Iyer was raised in both England and California, giving him a multicultural perspective that deeply influences his writing.

Unlike traditional travel writers who focus on landscapes, cuisine, or adventure, Iyer explores themes of significance with place, identity, belonging, and the intersection of cultures. He delves into how travel shapes the human soul, often writing about the emotional and spiritual aspects of movement and stillness.

Visit www.picoiyer.com

Born in Oxford, England, and raised amidst the rolling hills of Santa Barbara, California, Pico Iyer discovered the magic of movement. He would grow to become not just a travel writer but a philosopher of the open road. To call him a "travel writer" is akin to calling the Grand Canyon a ditch—technically accurate, yet so far from the full truth.

Pico Iyer's gift was not in recounting destinations or crafting glossy advertisements for far-flung resorts. No, his genius lay in something much deeper: revealing the landscapes of the human spirit through the lens of physical exploration. In his hands, travel became more than a journey from Point A to Point B. It was a pilgrimage, a practice, a portal to understanding oneself and the interconnectedness of the world. This is the story of how Pico Iyer transformed the art of wandering into a masterclass on being human.

Pico's books—*The Art of Stillness*, *The Open Road*, and *The Man Within My Head*—read like meditations. They invite us not to merely visit places but to inhabit them. He asks us to sit still in the whirlwind of our journeys and, in doing so, discover the profound truths hidden in the quiet corners of our souls.

In a world obsessed with speed, efficiency, and Instagram-worthy backdrops, Pico offered a different map—one charting the contours of mindfulness, identity, and belonging. He argued that travel was not about ticking landmarks off a list but about peeling back the layers of oneself in new and unfamiliar contexts.

Travel writing, before Pico, often focused on the external—the soaring spires of medieval cathedrals, the bustling marketplaces of Marrakech, or the verdant terraces of Bali. But Pico looked inward. For him, the most significant journeys occurred not on cobblestone streets or mountain trails but within the depths of the heart and mind. His narratives wove together reflections on identity, culture, and the meaning of home. And his words touched a nerve.

Readers found themselves moved not to book tickets but to reconsider their relationship with the world around them. In his hands, travel became a vehicle for self-discovery—a radical concept in an age of guidebooks promising "top 10" lists and "hacks" for every trip.

From our interview, Pico inspired us to champion mindful travel. Long before mindfulness became a buzzword, Pico was its quiet advocate. He spoke of the value of "slow travel," of taking the time to absorb a place, to engage deeply with its people and rhythms. His essays reminded us that the most meaningful journeys were not those where we collected souvenirs but where we returned home transformed.

This ethos resonated with travelers seeking something beyond the superficial. It inspired a movement toward intentional and experiential travel, away from the fast-paced itineraries of modern tourism. Pico's vision helped shape an industry now prioritizing authenticity over spectacle.

When you listen to the entire conversation with Pico, you will hear the voice of a global soul.

He describes himself as a man shaped by multiple cultures but rooted in none. This unique perspective allowed him to capture the beauty of cultural intersections. Whether writing about Japan's meditative temples, the chaos of Indian train stations, or the serenity of remote monasteries, Pico's lens was always one of reverence and curiosity.

Through his words, he bridged divides. He made the unfamiliar familiar and the mundane extraordinary. His sensitivity to cultural nuance challenged readers to approach the world with humility and respect. And in doing so, he became an advocate for responsible, thoughtful travel practices.

As a quiet revolutionary traveler, Pico never loudly championed sustainability, but his reverence for places and cultures carried an implicit message: preserve what makes a destination unique. Protect its spirit. By encouraging travelers to tread lightly and engage meaningfully, he became an unlikely yet profound voice for sustainable tourism.

Moreover, his storytelling—weaving history, politics, and personal introspection—elevated travel writing into an art form. He reminded us that every place carries stories waiting to be told, and every journey holds lessons waiting to be learned.

In an era where travel is often reduced to a commodity, Pico Iyer's work stands as a timeless reminder: travel is not about consumption but transformation. It's about connection—to people, to places, and to ourselves. His writings challenge us to move through the world with intention, to seek meaning over mileage, and to embrace the journey within as fervently as the journey without.

So the next time you pack a suitcase or board a plane, remember the significant message of Pico Iyer and his quiet invitation to explore not just the world but your place within it.

Enjoy the entire conversation with Pico Iyer on our *Success Made to Last* podcast by scanning this QR code.

24

SIGNIFICANCE OF A $10 LESSON

"Letting go isn't about giving up; it's about accepting that some things are beyond your control and making room for what can be."

~Robin Abb—The Downsizing Doula

Richard Birke – Visionary, Lawyer, JAMS Chief Architect

Richard Birke is the Executive Director for the JAMS Institute (Judicial Arbitration and Mediation Services). He was led to dispute resolution because it is inter-disciplinary, affecting every aspect of life. Richard believes that every conflict is an opportunity to learn, grow and become better. JAMS Pathway walks into situations with the objective of turning conflict into consensus, creating a pathway for all parties to optimize what ever it is they care about.

Visit www.jamsadr.com

It was an ordinary day for Richard Birke and his 11-year-old son. The two were walking together, en route to a much-anticipated event. Spirits were high until his son stopped abruptly, patting his pocket with a furrowed brow.

"Dad," he said, "I had two $10 bills, but now I can only find one. Can we go back home and look for the other one?"

Richard paused. And as fathers do, he recognized this moment wasn't just about a missing bill—it was about a lesson. One his son might carry for a lifetime.

"Son," Richard began, "this is one of those big moments in your life." The boy looked up, puzzled. What big moment? It was just $10. "You're thinking of yourself as a $20 person who's lost $10," Richard explained. "And now you're willing to ruin your day to go back, tear your room apart, and maybe—just maybe—find it. But think about it differently. What if you saw yourself as a $10 person with options instead?"

Options? The boy was listening now.

"If we go back, we lose our fun for the day. And even if we find the $10, the time and joy we've spent chasing it are worth more than that bill. Instead, you could choose to enjoy what you still have: the $10 in your pocket, this day, this moment. That's resetting your baseline, son. It's moving forward from where you are, not from where you *thought* you'd be."

His son stood there quietly for a moment, then nodded. They didn't go back to look for the money. They went on with their day, $10 lighter than planned but richer in understanding.

And that little lesson of perspective—the power of letting go and resetting—has echoed through Richard's life, not just as a father but as a leader, a mentor, and a conflict resolver.

Richard Birke is now the Chief Architect of JAMS Pathway (Judicial, Arbitration, Mediation Services), an organization dedicated to helping others navigate some of life's most complex disputes. His journey to this role is shaped by wisdom hard-earned and lessons deeply felt, including those from his own childhood.

Born to Holocaust survivors, Richard grew up surrounded by stories of unimaginable loss and resilience. His mother, with her third-grade education and unshakable optimism, taught him the simplest truths—like how to find beauty in every kind of weather. "Be nice, but don't be a sucker," she'd tell him. It's advice that's stayed with him as he mediates conflicts that would make most people's heads spin.

And spin they have. Over the years, Richard has found himself in the middle of everything from massive civil rights settlements to environmental battles involving timberland, jobs, and thousand-year-old trees. Through it all, his approach has been simple but profound: listen, be curious, and help others reset their baseline.

Because, as Richard knows better than most, conflicts often arise not because people don't care, but because they care *too much*—about the same thing, in different ways. And finding common ground starts not with what's been lost, but with what's still possible.

In his own words: "Success is about what you achieve. But significance? That's about what you contribute. At the end of the day, the question isn't how much money you have or what kind of car you drive. It's this: Did I help? Did I make a difference?"

And now, as a father, teacher, and mentor, Richard is passing that mindset on to the next generation—beginning with his son and a lesson worth far more than $10.

Enjoy the entire conversation with Richard Birke on *Success Made to Last* podcast by scanning this QR code.

25

SIGNIFICANCE OF HOLIDAY TRADITIONS

"Family traditions are the threads that weave generations together, grounding us in our roots while guiding us forward. At Christmas, these rituals remind us that true significance lies not in the gifts we give, but in the love, connection, and shared memories that endure."

~Life Lessons

Chanda Bell and Mom – Creators of The Elf on the Shelf

Chanda Bell is one of the co-creators of The Elf on the Shelf, a Christmas tradition that has become a global phenomenon. What makes Chanda Bell's contribution significant is how she and her family turned a simple childhood memory into a multimillion-dollar business without the backing of a major publisher. Through grassroots marketing and strategic partnerships, The Elf on the Shelf became a household name, leading to TV specials, merchandise, and even a balloon in the Macy's Thanksgiving Day Parade.

The success of the brand showcases the power of storytelling, entrepreneurship, and the ability to create lasting traditions.

Visit www.lumistella.com

Traditions serve as more than just dates on the calendar or occasions for celebration. They are, in many ways, our roadmaps—connecting us to the past and helping to guide us into the future. And when it comes to holiday traditions, few things have captured the imagination of children and families in recent memory quite like The Elf on the Shelf. But there's more to this tradition than just the mischievous antics of an elf.

Chanda Bell, co-creator of The Elf on the Shelf, would likely tell you that the magic lies not in the toy but in what it represents: a bridge between generations, a reminder of the values we hold dear, and a celebration of the wonder that comes with the Christmas season.

Now, let me take you back to a time, when the road wasn't so crowded, and Christmas was simpler, yet somehow fuller. You see, Chanda Bell didn't grow up in a mansion, but she was rich in the things that mattered: faith, family, and the gift of imagination. In the modest home where she was raised, Chanda's parents—who may not have had a lot to give materially—instilled in her a legacy of generosity, kindness, and belief in the things unseen.

As a child, she marveled at the magic of Christmas. Each year, an elf, one that her mother had known since her own childhood, would arrive, watching, listening, and returning to Santa every night to report on the happenings in the Bell household. It was a simple tradition, but as Chanda would tell you, it was nothing short of enchanting.

"We didn't have a lot, but that elf brought wonder," Chanda reflects. "He was a link to the North Pole, a connection to something bigger, something magical."

Fast forward to 2005, and The Elf on the Shelf was born—not just from a desire to create a book and a precious elf, but to pass on the joy of holiday traditions to a new generation. For Chanda, it was never just about the Christmas product, but about what the elf represented—time spent together as a family, the joy of shared moments, and the spark of excitement that lit up her childhood Christmases.

So what is it about traditions like The Elf on the Shelf that resonate so deeply with families today? Perhaps it's that in the fast-paced world we live in, these traditions give us permission to slow down. As Chanda might tell you, there's something grounding about gathering your family around, whether it's hunting for that cheeky elf or huddling up under blankets to watch a Christmas special together.

"The world is noisy," she says, "but holiday traditions quiet that noise, if only for a while."

Indeed, those fleeting moments—when a child's eyes light up, when families gather to bake cookies or hang ornaments—are more than just activities. They are memories in the making, signposts in the timeline of our lives. As Chanda remembers it, even the simplest of gifts, like the blue bicycle she received one Christmas, carried with it a lifetime of happiness. It wasn't about the material things—it was about the feeling of being loved and cherished.

That's the thing about traditions. They stay with us. Whether it's the smell of your grandmother's broccoli casserole wafting through the air on Thanksgiving, or the memory of learning to ride your first bike, these moments stitch together the tapestry of our lives.

And perhaps, most significantly, traditions offer us something else—a way to teach. The elf, after all, isn't just a game of hide and seek; it's a lesson in self-control, generosity, and kindness. Each year, millions of children across the world are reminded that kindness, good behavior, and giving to others are values worth celebrating, not just at Christmas, but all year round.

Chanda Bell, whose family now works tirelessly to ensure The Elf on the Shelf continues to be a source of joy for families everywhere, understands that the holiday tradition is not only about creating fun but about building a legacy. "My daughter's college roommates told me, 'You made our childhood.'" That's no small feat.

But, for Chanda, the true legacy she hopes to leave goes beyond the elf. At the heart of her message is something much deeper—something she wants her children and all families to remember above all else: faith. "Jesus first," she says with conviction. "That is the only thing that will last."

As you prepare for the holidays this year and gather around to pass down your own family traditions—whether they involve an elf, a special meal, or simply spending time with loved ones—remember this: these moments of significance are not just about the celebration. They are about connection. They are about faith. And they are about love.

Enjoy the entire conversation with Chanda on *Success Made to Last* podcast by scanning the QR code.

26

SIGNIFICANCE OF BREAKING GLASS CEILINGS

"If your actions inspire others to dream more, learn more, do more, and become more, you are a leader."
~President John Quincy Adams

Neomosha Nelson – Advocate for the People

Neomosha Nelson is a seasoned professional with extensive experience in diversity, equity, and inclusion, nonprofit management, legal research and writing, and event management. She has made her mark in bringing communities together, dating back to 1973 when she was elected the first African American female as Student Body President in Sherman, Texas.

In a time of social upheaval and seismic cultural shifts, a quiet revolution was brewing in Sherman, Texas. It was 1973. The Civil Rights Movement was in the rearview mirror, yet its echoes were far from silent in this small North Texas town. The year would prove monumental, not just for the town, but for one extraordinary young woman.

Her name? Neomosha Nelson.

She was not just qualified to lead; she was, by all accounts, overqualified. Yet, the role she stepped into wasn't merely about academic accolades or organizational finesse. No, this was bigger. She became the first African American and the first woman elected Student Body President of Sherman High School. A double glass ceiling, shattered in a single vote.

Neomosha didn't just preside over her classmates. She became a symbol—a beacon of progress in a community navigating the tenuous waters of desegregation. And while many would have seen the role as the apex of achievement, for Neomosha, it was just the beginning.

Fast forward through the years, and her path led her to law school, the courtrooms of Philadelphia, and into academia. But the journey was not without trials—literal and figurative.

In her own words: "I'm not the person I was before. I'll never be that person again."

You see, life threw its sharpest daggers at her. A diagnosis of Crohn's colitis led to emergency surgeries and weeks in a coma. She awoke to a life altered forever. Eighteen inches of her colon were gone, her body marked by the scalpel of survival. The medications were blurring, but what life took, it also gave back in perspective.

She learned to treasure time—because, as she'll tell you, "it's precious." She learned to reconnect with family, weaving tighter bonds with those who share her bloodline. And she turned to teaching, not for prestige but for impact, molding young minds in places where her voice could make a difference.

Her leadership style? Synthesizing conversations, building bridges, finding common ground. Her Achilles heel? Procrastination—she laughs as she admits it. But even that, she's turned into a life lesson: don't let overthinking paralyze action.

And when asked about her defining moments, she recounts a bold pivot—a "hell yeah" decision to leave the familiar for the unknown. Philadelphia became her proving ground, broadening her view of the world and opening doors she hadn't imagined.

So, what's next for Neomosha Nelson? Sharing her knowledge through teaching? Because as she wisely says, "What's the point of having it if I don't pass it on?"

But here's the part of the story that matters most: Neomosha Nelson never saw herself as extraordinary. She simply saw the gaps—racial, gendered, generational—and set out to bridge them. She doesn't dwell on the obstacles; she focuses on the significance.

From a Student Body President of Sherman High to a seasoned woman of wisdom, Neomosha's life is a testament to resilience, service, and the relentless pursuit of meaning.

Enjoy the entire conversation with Neomosha Nelson on *Success Made to Last* podcast by scanning this QR code.

27

SIGNIFICANCE OF A DIFFERENCE MAKER

"Waste no more time arguing about what a good man should be. Be one."

~Marcus Aurelius

Bill McCartney – Founder of Promise Keepers

Bill McCartney was the head football coach at the University of Colorado from 1982 to 1994, leading the Buffaloes to a national championship in 1990. Beyond his success on the field, he was also the founder of the Christian men's organization Promise Keepers, which became a nationwide movement promoting faith-based values and men's leadership in family and society.

His legacy of significance is a blend of football excellence and faith-driven activism.

Visit www.promisekeepers.org

In early 2025, we received word that Coach Bill McCartney had passed away. We knew Bill and his son, Tom, who coached at Fairview High School in Boulder, Colorado, where our daughters attended. He was a wonderful dad, grandfather, friend, and a man of football. The fiery head coach of the University of Colorado, he built a program that went from underdog to top dog, achieving college football's ultimate prize: a national championship in 1990. His name became synonymous with gridiron greatness. But there's a significant chapter of McCartney's life that few know—a chapter not about Xs and Os, but about hearts and souls.

Let me take you back to the late 1980s. McCartney was at the height of his career, leading the Buffaloes to national prominence. Across state lines, in Nebraska, there was Ricky Simmons—a once-promising wide receiver for the Cornhuskers. Simmons had all the talent in the world, but his life took a tragic turn. After his football career ended, he spiraled into drug addiction, eventually finding himself behind bars for drug distribution.

It would've been easy for most to write Simmons off as just another cautionary tale. But not Bill McCartney. When he heard about Simmons' struggles, McCartney didn't shake his head in judgment or walk away. He leaned in.

The decorated coach, known for his fiery sideline demeanor, quietly began visiting Simmons in prison. He wasn't there to talk football. He wasn't there to lecture. McCartney came as a man of faith, offering something Simmons had long since stopped expecting from the world: compassion.

Ricky Simmons later admitted he was stunned. Why would a man like McCartney, a national figure, care about someone like him—someone who'd seemingly wasted every opportunity? But McCartney wasn't interested in Simmons' past. He was invested in his future.

McCartney spoke about forgiveness, redemption, and the God of second chances. He wasn't preaching at Simmons—he was walking alongside him. And step by step, those prison visits began to change Simmons' outlook. When Simmons was released, he didn't just turn his life around—he became a motivational speaker, using his story to help others escape the grip of addiction.

But this story doesn't stop there. McCartney's compassion for Ricky Simmons wasn't an isolated act. It was part of a larger mission that would soon take shape. On the field, McCartney was known for uniting players from every background—black, white, rich, poor, urban, rural—calling team meetings to tackle hard conversations about race and unity.

In 1990, shortly after his championship season, McCartney founded *Promise Keepers*, a men's ministry dedicated to fostering faith, accountability, and reconciliation across racial and cultural lines. Its heartbeat? The same belief that drove him to Simmons' prison cell: the idea that every man matters and that unity is a calling higher than competition.

Bill McCartney's career may have been defined by the scoreboard, but his legacy? That was written in places far from stadium lights—in prisons, in locker rooms, and in the lives of people like Ricky Simmons.

So, the next time you hear his name, don't just think of championships or the roar of the crowd. Think of the quiet moments of compassion, the belief in second chances, and the power of reconciliation. Here's to Coach Mac—a significant difference maker!

Enjoy more of the story on *Success Made to Last* podcast by scanning this QR code.

28

SIGNIFICANCE OF BELIEVING IN POTENTIAL

"Leadership is about serving others, not being served."
~Tom Osborne

Tom Osborne – Coach of the Decade, Congressman, Husband,
Dad, Granddad, Mentor

Tom Osborne was the head football coach at the University of
Nebraska from 1973 to 1997, leading the Cornhuskers to three
national championships (1994, 1995, and 1997). He was known
for his innovative offensive strategies, particularly the powerful
option running game, and for maintaining one of the most dom-
inant programs in college football history.

Beyond coaching, Osborne served as a U.S. Congressman
(R-Nebraska) from 2001 to 2007 and later as Nebraska's Ath-
letic Director from 2007 to 2013. He is widely respected for his
leadership, integrity, and significant impact on both athletics and
public service.

Vist www.teammates.org

43,000 young lives transformed. Across five states. That's the ripple effect of the TeamMates Mentoring Program—a vision born in 1991 from the hearts of Dr. Tom Osborne and his wife, Nancy. Together, they embarked on a mission to inspire students to reach their full potential through the power of mentorship. But to understand the program's impact, you must first understand the man behind it.

Coach Tom Osborne. A name synonymous with excellence, purpose, and integrity. Best known as the legendary head coach of the Nebraska Cornhuskers football team and named National Coach of the Decade in the 1990s, Osborne's influence extended far beyond the gridiron. His greatest victories weren't measured in touchdowns or trophies but in lives changed—especially those of underprivileged youth.

Throughout his coaching career, Osborne was a mentor, a guide, and a father figure to countless young black athletes who faced daunting socioeconomic challenges. He didn't just coach them to win games; he coached them to win at life. Discipline, persever-ance, teamwork—these were the values he instilled, values that transcended football. Osborne's profound empathy and unwavering belief in the potential of every individual enabled him to help young men overcome obstacles and build brighter futures.

And yet, Osborne's influence didn't stop at the locker room door. In 1991, alongside his wife Nancy, he co-founded the TeamMates Mentoring Program. What began as a small initiative pairing caring adults with at-risk youth grew into one of the nation's most respected mentoring programs. The ripple effect? Far-reaching and profound.

Mentees in the program experience remarkable growth. Their school attendance improves, their grades rise, and their chances of graduating high school soar. Many go on to pursue higher education or vocational training, inspired by the guidance and encouragement of their mentors. Beyond academics, they develop confidence and resilience, empowered to overcome life's challenges with a steady hand of support by their side.

But it's not just the mentees who grow. Mentors often describe the experience as life-changing. They find a renewed sense of purpose, a deeper connection to their communities, and the fulfillment that comes from investing in the next generation. The act of giving, they discover, is a gift in itself.

The impact extends to strengthening families, too. As mentees gain confidence, they become role models for their own families, creating a cycle of mentorship that spans generations. Improved self-esteem and outlook often lead to better family dynamics, fostering unity and hope.

The program had community-wide impact. Entire communities feel the ripple. Dropout rates fall. Local economies benefit from a more skilled workforce. A culture of service and connectivity emerges, uniting people from all walks of life under a shared mission.

Perhaps the most inspiring ripple of all: many former mentees become mentors themselves. They pay it forward, creating a legacy of service and support that continues to grow. By addressing challenges like educational disparities and youth disconnection, the program ensures opportunities for future generations.

Today, the TeamMates Mentoring Program serves over 10,000 students annually, a testament to the enduring power of Osborne's vision and compassion. And yet, this was only one chapter of his remarkable life.

After retiring from coaching, Osborne took his values to Washington, D.C., serving three terms as a U.S. Congressman from Nebraska (2001–2007). True to form, Osborne's tenure in Congress was marked by integrity and a commitment to bipartisan problem-solving. He tackled issues like education, youth development, and healthcare, always prioritizing the common good over party lines. In a time of division, he built bridges. In a place of noise, he led with quiet strength.

Tom Osborne's legacy is one of character, faith, and servant leadership. His actions remind us that true success isn't about accolades or achievements but about the lives we touch and the significant difference we make. Whether mentoring young athletes, shaping policy, or inspiring communities, Osborne's life is a testament to the power of selfless service and unwavering principles.

Enjoy the entire conversation with Tom Osborne on *Success Made to Last* podcast by scanning this OR code.

The Inventors

29

SIGNIFICANCE OF CHANGING LIVES THROUGH DESIGN

"Girls must grow up knowing they can do anything, especially through imaginative design."

~Sofie Roux

Sofie Roux – Designer, Entrepreneur, Founder of Bloombox,
Visionary

Sofie Roux is the founder and CEO of BloomBox Design Labs, a company dedicated to expanding access to STEAM education through innovative, sustainable design. At just 19 years old, she has been recognized as a visionary Gen Z leader transforming education through her commitment to social impact.

Sofie's passion for education and innovation has led her to develop the SuperBloom Global Knowledge Network App, set to launch Spring 2025. This platform aims to connect students worldwide through short videos addressing their big questions, furthering her mission to make education accessible and engaging for all.

Visit www.bloomboxdesignlab.com

Sofie Roux's story doesn't begin where you might think. Not in a boardroom or a bustling startup, but in Vancouver—a place where nature whispers its secrets to those willing to listen. Among the towering mountains and endless ocean, Sofie's dreams took shape. She was just a child then, with wide eyes and a sketchbook, but even then, the seeds of something extraordinary were sprouting.

Raised in a household of strong, determined women, Sofie didn't just learn to dream; she learned to act. It was her mother who taught her that limits were meant to be broken, that the only ceiling was the sky. And Sofie has been reaching for it ever since.

At just 19 years old, Sofie Roux is not your ordinary college sophomore. She's a founder. A CEO. A visionary. But most importantly, she's a builder—not just of structures, but of futures. Through her company, BloomBox Design Labs, Sofie is proving that one innovative idea can reshape lives.

You see, her journey began long before her first day at Stanford. It started with glitter and glue, with a project called "Sparkly and Smart." Most kids sell lemonade or cookies. Sofie? She raised $300,000—yes, you heard that right—to support girls' education. She wasn't even old enough to drive, but she was already paving the road for others.

Then came the trip to Malawi. It was supposed to be a celebration—a chance to see the fruits of her efforts firsthand. But as she rode into the village on a dusty truck, surrounded by the joy of children and the gratitude of families, something shifted. The tears came, uninvited but undeniable. Sofie saw not just what was missing, but what *could be.*

And that's when BloomBox Design Labs was born. Not in a fancy office or with a multimillion-dollar investment, but in the heart of a girl who dared to dream big. BloomBoxes are more than solar-powered computer labs made from repurposed shipping containers—they are hope wrapped in steel and sunlight.

Sofie's vision isn't just about providing tools; it's about unlocking potential. These BloomBoxes are built for the kids who've never had access to electricity, let alone the internet. They're for the teachers who want to inspire but lack the resources to do so. They're for the communities that dream of a better tomorrow but need a little help to get there.

But Sofie's not doing this alone. Her mom, who now leads logistics, is her greatest ally. Her mentors provide wisdom, her team contributes brilliance, and the students she serves remind her why she started.

Now, let me tell you something about Sofie Roux. She's not just an entrepreneur. She's a designer who believes every challenge hides an opportunity. She's a collaborator who knows that the best ideas come from listening, not talking. She's a Gen Z leader who's rewriting the rules of what's possible.

And while Sofie juggles classes at Stanford with running a global impact enterprise, she dreams even bigger. She envisions a world where sustainability and education go hand in hand, where every child has the tools to create their own destiny, and where girls grow up knowing they can be anything—*anything*.

But here's the best part. Sofie's story isn't finished. Far from it. She's just getting started. More BloomBoxes. More partnerships. More lives changed.

Enjoy the entire conversation with Sofie Roux on *Success Made to Last* podcast by scanning this QR code.

30

SIGNIFICANCE OF ENLIGHTENED DETERMINATION

"A candle loses nothing by lighting another candle."
~James Keller

Alice Min Soo Chun – Inventor, Architect, Professor, Visionary

Alice Min Soo Chun is a pioneering inventor and social entrepreneur known for her work in sustainable design and solar technology. She is the inventor of the SolarPuff, the world's first self-inflating, portable solar lantern, designed to provide clean, renewable light to people in disaster-stricken and off-grid areas.

Her innovation has helped communities affected by natural disasters, such as those in Haiti after the 2010 earthquake and in Puerto Rico following Hurricane Maria.

Visit www.solight-design.com

Alice Min Soo Chun's story is one of resilience, invention, and a light that refuses to dim. Born in Seoul, South Korea, Alice came into the world under the weight of impoverished circumstances. At just four years old, she and her family immigrated to the United States, settling in a struggling neighborhood outside of Syracuse, New York. The transition was anything but smooth. Alice found herself marginalized, the only Asian in her school, subject to bullying and alienation. But even as a child, Alice learned to fight—not with fists, but with an inner light that shone through her imagination and determination.

She carried that light through her education, eventually earning a graduate degree from the University of Pennsylvania. Her academic journey led her to teaching architecture at prestigious institutions like Columbia University, the University of Pennsylvania, and even lecturing at MIT and Harvard. It was while teaching at Columbia that her path took an unexpected turn. Alice became captivated by solar energy and material technology—a passion born out of personal necessity.

When her son was born, Alice spent countless hours in doctors' offices, observing the alarming rates of childhood asthma and eczema. Her research revealed a devastating truth: one in four children suffers from asthma, a condition exacerbated by pollution from energy consumption in buildings. Seventy-five percent of air pollution stems from heating, cooling, and lighting systems. The more she learned, the more determined she became. Alice turned her expertise in material technology toward a singular mission: creating sustainable solutions to combat environmental and health crises.

Alice's ingenuity took form in her solar technology. Drawing inspiration from her childhood lessons in origami, she began sewing solar panels onto thin fabrics, designing lightweight and flexible prototypes. When the catastrophic earthquake struck Haiti in 2010, Alice felt an undeniable call to action. Her research had

139

uncovered another sobering statistic: 2.6 billion people worldwide live without electricity, relying instead on toxic, costly kerosene. This deadly fuel not only pollutes but also causes fires and respiratory illnesses, claiming the lives of millions annually.

With a rudimentary prototype in hand, made from duct tape and glue, Alice attended a tech expo in Haiti, sponsored by the Clinton Foundation. There, she demonstrated her invention—a solar light that folded flat and expanded into a functional, elegant cube. Its simplicity and beauty captured the attention of President Bill Clinton and the President of Haiti. Their encouragement propelled Alice to refine her design, ultimately leading to the SolarPuff, an origami-inspired solar light that has since illuminated the lives of millions.

Alice's lights have brought hope and safety to disaster-stricken areas worldwide. When Hurricane Maria devastated Puerto Rico, leaving three million people without power, Alice and her team delivered over 100,000 SolarPuffs to those in need. She's traveled to Dominica, Ukraine, and beyond, delivering light to children in makeshift schools, hospitals, and refugee camps. In Ukraine, where war has left countless children traumatized, Alice's colorful lights have been used for PTSD therapy, offering comfort and calm in the darkest of times.

Her work caught the attention of global leaders and innovators. Hillary Clinton included Alice in her book *The Book of Gutsy Women*, placing her alongside icons like Jane Goodall and Greta Thunberg. The story didn't end there; Clinton's Apple TV docuseries *Gutsy* brought Alice's mission to an even wider audience. Bob Iger, Disney's CEO, also lent his support, helping Alice deliver lights to Ukrainian children affected by the ongoing war.

Alice's journey is a testament to the power of perseverance and imagination. From a childhood shaped by hardship to a career defined by innovation, she has never lost sight of her guiding principle: that even the smallest acts of kindness can ripple outward, creating profound change. She teaches children not just to dream but to believe in the transformative power of their own inner light. "The sun is the most powerful source of energy that comes to Earth every day," she tells them, "but the light of your heart and your mind is even more powerful."

Alice Chun's life reminds us that beauty, wonder, and awe are not just luxuries but necessities. In the face of darkness, her creations bring light—literal and metaphorical—to those who need it most.

Enjoy the entire conversation with Alice Chun on *Success Made to Last* podcast by scanning this QR code.

31

SIGNIFICANCE OF FEARLESSNESS

"Hope lies in dreams, in imagination, and in the courage of those who dare to make dreams into reality."

~Dr. Jonas Salk

Regina Herzlinger – Entrepreneur, Author, First Woman Dean at Harvard Business School

Regina Herzlinger is a truly significant figure in healthcare policy and innovation. Often called the "Godmother of Consumer-Driven Healthcare," she was the first woman to be tenured at Harvard Business School and the first woman Dean at Harvard Business School. Her groundbreaking work has influenced how policymakers, business leaders, and academics think about healthcare reform, emphasizing transparency, patient choice, and market-driven solutions. Of note, Regina was the first faculty member to be selected by the students as their best instructor.

Together with her husband, an MIT Ph.D. physicist, they co-invented medical devices, including blood circulation pumps, that have saved hundreds of thousands of lives.

She was born in a land of conflict, where the echoes of war were as common as the sound of the sea. A little girl, no older than five, would stare at the bullet holes in the stucco walls of her home—not with fear, but with curiosity. She wondered about the trajectory, the force, the physics behind them.

Somewhere between those war-torn streets of Israel and the hallowed halls of Harvard, Regina Herzlinger learned something priceless: Fearlessness.

It was that very fearlessness that led her to do what no woman had done before—become the first tenured female professor at the Harvard Business School. And not just tenured—CHAIR. The first woman to sit at the helm of one of the world's most prestigious institutions for business education.

Ah, but her battle wasn't only academic. No, she took on an even mightier beast—one that confounded scholars and economists alike. A beast with a name we all know: Healthcare. Decades before politicians and pundits argued over its future, Regina had already seen its unraveling. Managed care was on borrowed time, she warned. The future belonged to the consumer.

When nobody had the right term for it—she gave them one: *Consumer-driven healthcare.* It was an idea so radical, so controversial, that it turned heads—and raised voices.

But that's Regina. She never backed down from a challenge. She wrote the books, literally, on how to fix healthcare. *Market-Driven Healthcare* was her grenade tossed into the status quo. It didn't just make waves—it caused a storm. And while critics balked at the idea of consumers having a greater voice, time proved her right. Telemedicine, direct-to-consumer health innovations, patient-centered care—ideas once dismissed as fantasy are now mainstream reality.

But there's more to Regina's story.

Alongside her husband—an MIT physicist—she built companies. Not just any companies. Companies that saved lives. One of their crowning achievements? A device that can replace all of a bleeding patient's blood in just minutes.

Life-saving. Battlefield-tested. Revolutionary.

And when war once again ravaged the streets of another country—Ukraine—Regina did what she always does. She took action. She and her husband sent 30 of their rapid infusers to the front lines, ensuring that soldiers—no matter their uniform—had a fighting chance.

Today, Regina is far from done.

She holds patents for new medical devices. She's writing yet another book—this time, a blueprint on how to *actually* innovate in healthcare. Not theory. Not wishful thinking. Real, actionable change.

Her secret? She thinks BIG. She mentors. She measures success not by accolades, but by impact. And when someone tells her *no*, she doesn't retreat. She educates them on why they're wrong.

Because as she once learned, "No" just means they haven't yet realized how good her idea is—for *them*.

Listen to the entire conversation with Regina Herzlinger on *Success Made to Last* podcast by scanning this QR code.

32

SIGNIFICANCE OF BEING CHILDLIKE

"In a world where you can be anything, be kind."
~Heather Barnes

Jim Henson, Puppeteer

Jim Henson's vision was not just about creating funny characters or entertaining children, but about using puppetry to communicate universal themes of listening, grace, love, empathy, kindness, and understanding. His work on *Sesame Street* and *The Muppet Show* helped shape how we think about childhood education and entertainment, showing that humor, joy, and meaningful lessons could go hand-in-hand.

His belief that entertainment could be both fun and educational transformed the way we see puppetry, making it a powerful form of storytelling that resonates deeply with people of all ages, as witnessed by the puppet theatre we built our children and grandchildren.

That's significant.

147

He was just a boy from Greenville, Mississippi. A shy dreamer, with his head in the clouds and his hands often full of felt and string. Young Jim Henson didn't want to be famous. He wasn't chasing the limelight or the applause. No, Jim wanted to make people smile—genuinely, innocently, and wholeheartedly.

His journey began not in the grand halls of Hollywood but on a small local TV show. A green sock turned into a frog. A frog that would one day leap from local screens to prime-time stardom. That frog, of course, was Kermit. And with Kermit came a motley crew of unlikely heroes: a diva pig, a nervous bear, and a cookie-obsessed monster. Each one became a reflection of us all—our quirks, our dreams, our flaws.

But Jim wasn't just building puppets. He was building a bridge— a bridge to imagination. You see, he believed that laughter could heal and that kindness could be taught. He understood that the simplest lessons, delivered through a fuzzy friend, could change a child's world.

He once said, "The most sophisticated people I know—inside, they are all children." And so, he created worlds where that inner child could feel safe, seen, and loved. *Sesame Street* taught us how to count and spell, but it also taught us about friendship and empathy. *The Muppet Show* gave us belly laughs, but it also reminded us that even misfits could create something magical together.

But Jim's creativity wasn't confined to puppets. It was in his storytelling, his belief in the power of wonder. Whether he was crafting a labyrinth of fantasy or taking us to a dark crystal world, Jim Henson dared us to dream bigger. He gave us permission to believe that a frog could talk, that monsters could love cookies, and that the world was full of possibilities.

When Jim Henson passed away at just 53, the world mourned a man whose work had touched millions. But Jim didn't leave behind an empire—he left a legacy. A legacy of joy, of creativity, and of significance. For Jim Henson's true genius was not in his ability to entertain, but in his ability to connect.

Today, when you hear Kermit's banjo or see Big Bird's wide wings, remember: Jim Henson didn't just show us a world of puppets. He showed us the best of ourselves, the most significant of being childlike.

To hear our tribute to Jim Henson, scan this QR code.

33

SIGNIFICANCE OF COLLABORATING

"My strength does not come from me alone, but from many."
~Māori Proverb (New Zealand)

Johnny Mercer – Oscar and Grammy Winner, Founder of
Capitol Records

Johnny Mercer was a truly significant figure in American music, known for his extraordinary contributions as a lyricist, composer, and singer. He co-founded Capitol Records and wrote some of the most memorable songs of the 20th century, including classics like "Moon River," "Charade," "The Days of Wine and Roses," "Autumn Leaves," "That Old Black Magic," and "Hooray for Hollywood."

Johnny's unique ability to blend poetic lyrics with melodic innovation helped shape the American Songbook and left a lasting impact on jazz, pop, and film music. His legacy as a master of both lyricism and melody continues to inspire musicians and songwriters around the world.

Visit www.johnnymercerfoundation.org

Johnny Mercer is the name behind some of the most unforget-table lyrics in American music history. A man who captured the essence of life, love, and longing in a way few could. But behind those words, behind the melodies that defined an era, there was something else—something deeper. A truth that, perhaps, even Johnny himself might have considered his greatest gift: the art of collaboration.

His niece, Nancy Mercer Giraud, a dear friend of ours, spoke of her uncle Bubba with fondness and a touch of longing. We had the privilege of visiting her in Savannah, where she painted a picture of Mercer that few ever saw. Not just the celebrated lyricist, but the man—the storyteller. And in those stories, she revealed something truly remarkable.

He was born in Savannah in 1909, growing up around music. As a toddler, Johnny's parents sang to him often and took him to minstrel and vaudeville shows. He grew up singing in church choirs, played trumpet and piano, and frequented local dance halls. As jazz was emerging in the 1920s, he heard the most vibrant, innovative sounds from African Americans and the Gullah from the local coast. His deeply Southern upbringing would later give Johnny's lyrics that unique down-home charm.

Take the line from "Moon River"—"my huckleberry friend." You see, that wasn't just poetic whimsy. That was Johnny, as a boy, picking huckleberries down a dusty road, lost in the rhythm of nature's song. A simple, fleeting moment that, years later, became immortalized in music. But inspiration, dear reader, is only part of the story.

Johnny Mercer's genius wasn't forged in solitude. No, it flour-ished in the company of others.

It was an evening in Hollywood, 1942. Hoagy Carmichael, the maestro behind "Stardust," sat at the piano. Johnny Mercer, the poet, leaned against the bar. Someone in the room threw out a challenge—why not write a song right here, right now?

Carmichael struck up a melody, light and playful. Mercer grabbed a napkin and began scribbling. In just a few hours, the world had a new tune—"In the Cool, Cool, Cool of the Evening." A song born not from long deliberation, but from the sheer magic of two minds in perfect sync. And it won an Academy Award, proving once again that the best creations are often the ones that simply...happen.

But collaboration wasn't just about camaraderie—it was about transformation. Just ask Ella Fitzgerald.

It was 1942 again, and Mercer had an idea—a song wrapped in allure, mystery, and romance. "That Old Black Magic." He had the words, Harold Arlen had the melody, but something was missing. Then Ella stepped into the studio. And when she sang, Mercer knew. The words he had penned now had a heartbeat, a soul. Fitzgerald took Mercer's lyrics and turned them into something ethereal, something eternal.

That was Johnny Mercer's gift. He saw the world not just as it was, but as it could be—with the right people, in the right moment. His legacy isn't just the songs he left behind, but the partnerships, the friendships, the collaborations that made 1,200 songs possible.

As Nancy would tell us, Mercer wasn't just a songwriter. He was a visionary. He didn't just write the music of his generation—he made sure the world could hear it. In 1942, he co-founded Capitol Records, giving voice to artists who might have otherwise remained unheard. He understood that music wasn't just about notes and lyrics—it was about people.

Johnny Mercer knew something that we often forget: that two are better than one. That in the harmony of collaboration, in the interplay of minds and talents, something greater emerges.

Enjoy the entire conversation with Nancy Mercer Giraud on *Success Made to Last* podcast clicking this QR code.

153

THE FUTURISTS

34

SIGNIFICANCE OF REDISCOVERING
YOUR PURPOSE

"Life isn't just about what we've lost. It's about what we still have to give, to experience, and to share."

~*Life Lessons*

Ed Asner – Emmy Award Winning Actor

Ed Asner, left a legacy of impactful performances, unwavering activism, and compassionate advocacy. His life exemplified a commitment to lifting others up—a quality that aligns with the idea of living a "truly significant" life. Across his career, we enjoyed his portrayals as Lou Grant, Santa Claus, and the irrepressible Carl Fredricksen in *UP*.

We were very lucky to know Ed and enjoy one of his final interviews.

Picture a quiet old man with black, square-framed glasses. His name is Carl Fredricksen. He sits in his worn chair, in a house filled with echoes—the memories of a life shared with Ellie, the love of his life. Their dreams, once as big as the sky, have been reduced to the square footage of their home. Carl clings to that house, to its peeling paint and sagging gutters, because it's not just wood and nails; it's Ellie. It's their story. And now, it's all he has left.

But Carl is not real. He is the creation of Pixar's animated masterpiece, *Up*, a film directed by Pete Docter. And yet, Carl is very real in another sense, because the man who gave him his voice, Ed Asner, knew Carl's pain all too well.

Ed Asner, a man whose voice was as rich and textured as the stories he told, was no stranger to loss. He'd climbed the peaks of Hollywood success, earning seven Emmy awards and the hearts of millions as Lou Grant. But as the years went by, Asner faced an uphill battle of a different kind. Aging. Relevance. Staying in the spotlight in an industry that often turns its back on those with silver in their hair.

When Asner took on the role of Carl, it was more than acting. It was an expression of his own journey—a man who, like Carl, had felt the sting of being put out to pasture. Carl's gruff demeanor and aching loneliness mirrored struggles Asner himself had faced. Hollywood can be unkind to its elders, and Asner knew this truth too well. But he never stopped fighting. He used his platform, his voice, and his passion to stay in the game, proving that age is no barrier to significance.

Through Carl, Asner delivered a performance that resonated across generations. Carl's story in *Up* begins in grief, as he mourns the loss of Ellie. He shuts himself off from the world, just as the world seems to have moved on without him. But then, a knock on the door—a persistent young boy named Russell—forces Carl to open his heart again. Together, they embark on an adventure that reminds Carl, and all of us, that life doesn't end with loss. It continues. And it can still be beautiful.

For Ed Asner, this story wasn't just a script; it was a credo. He, too, believed that life's most meaningful adventures could happen at any age. He refused to be defined by the passage of time or the fading spotlight. He continued to act, to advocate, and to inspire until his final days in 2021.

And here is the great lesson of *Up*: It's never too late to rediscover purpose. To let go of the past without letting go of love. To open the door to new connections, even when the world feels cold and distant. Carl found this truth, and in doing so, he soared—literally and metaphorically.

So, as the credits roll on both *Up* and the remarkable life of Ed Asner, we're left with a message that lingers long after the screen goes dark. Life isn't just about what we've lost. It's about what we still have to give, to experience, and to share.

Enjoy hearing the entire conversation with Ed Asner on *Success Made to Last* podcast by scanning the QR code.

35

SIGNIFICANCE OF CONSERVATION FOR ALL

"Being a social entrepreneur is often a journey of hills and valleys, and very fulfilling if you always keep your goals of significance in sight."

~Dr. Gladys Kalema-Zikusoka

Dr. Gladys Kalema-Zikusoka – Uganda's First African Woman
Wildlife Veterinarian

Gladys Kalema-Zikusoka, DVM, is Uganda's first wildlife veterinarian. She is the Founder of Conservation Through Public Health.

In her book, *Walking With Gorillas, The Journey of An African Wildlife Vet*, what begins as her enchanting account of being fresh out of vet school, treating sick gorillas, relocating wandering elephants, reintroducing giraffes, rescuing orphaned baby chimpanzees, and testing Cape buffalo for zoonotic diseases, becomes a tale of human health advocacy.

Gladys had a "moment of significant clarity" when she realized that in order to save the animals from extinction, we must also help our human neighbors. Making the connection that diseases in the local human communities are affecting gorillas and that tuberculosis is rampant in wild buffalo herds as well as among villagers, propelled Gladys forward to create a parallel path to improving health and well-being of the entire eco-system surrounding the Bwindi Impenetrable National Park. Thus, the NGO Conservation Through Public Health was born.

Visit www.ctph.org

It is said that, "We should aspire to be like the mountain gorillas: gentle, graceful, intelligent, and vulnerable." Those words belong to Dr. Gladys Kalema-Zikusoka, a woman whose life story reads like a testament to the very values she admires in these majestic creatures.

Growing up in Uganda, Gladys' father traveled the world serving as the Minister of Commerce and Industry. After Idi Amin overthrew the government, her father was targeted, kidnapped, and murdered during the turbulent regime. It was a turning point for Gladys' Mom, Rhoda, and her siblings. Gladys was only two.

At the age of four, Gladys' journey in wildlife began. During a visit to relatives in England, her Mom took Gladys to the London Zoo. Gladys made her career intentions known in a most memorable way, insisting on riding an elephant despite being far too young. This little girl had an unstoppable big dream—to become a wildlife veterinarian.

With an unwavering sense of purpose, Gladys attended the Royal Veterinary College in London, where she honed the skills that would define her life's work, becoming Uganda's first female wildlife veterinarian.

After returning to her homeland in 1996, she began caring for one of the world's most endangered species—the mountain gorillas. At that time, there were only 650 of these magnificent creatures left in the wild. Thanks to Gladys and her tireless efforts, that number has grown to over 1,000 today.

But it was more than just the numbers that defined her mission. The mountain gorillas taught her lessons that transcended science, lessons about the fragile balance of life, the interconnectedness of all beings, and the dignity that every living creature deserves.

One gorilla, in particular, left an indelible mark on Gladys' life. His name was Ruhondeza, a silverback whose calm and gentle nature became the cornerstone of Uganda's gorilla tourism. It was his demeanor that allowed Ruhondeza to live alongside humans peacefully, even as his strength waned in his later years.

161

According to Gladys, over 50,000 humans encountered Ruhondeza at his home in the Bwindi Impenetrable Forest.

In 2012, when Ruhondeza could no longer keep up with his troop, he sought refuge among the very people he had once kept at a distance. When Gladys found him, peacefully blending into the community, she realized something profound: Ruhondeza, this once-mighty silverback, felt safer among humans than in the wild he had called home for so long.

The villagers, guided by their own wisdom and compassion, decided to welcome Ruhondeza into their community. They allowed him to spend his final days cared for by the people whose lives he had touched.

And so it was that Ruhondeza, this gentle giant, passed away not in the isolation of the forest, but in the embrace of a community that had come to respect and honor him.

Dr. Gladys Kalema-Zikusoka, with the heart of a healer and the soul of a conservationist, reminds us all that true greatness lies not in power or dominance, but in gentleness, grace, intelligence, and vulnerability—the qualities that define the mountain gorillas she so dearly cares for.

These same qualities of gentleness, grace, intelligence with a strong dose of devoted love, define the significance of Dr. Gladys Kalema-Zikusoka.

To learn more about Gladys' groundbreaking work in saving endangered mountain gorillas and improving the health of the communities that live alongside them, visit www.ctph.org.

Enjoy the entire conversation on *Success Made to Last* podcast with Dr. Gladys Kalema-Zikusoka by scanning the QR code.

36

SIGNIFICANCE OF GREAT STORYTELLING

*"You can't travel the back roads very long without discovering
a multitude of gentle people doing good for others with no expectation of gain or recognition. The everyday kindness of the back
roads more than makes up for the acts of greed in the headlines.
Some people out there spend their whole lives selflessly."*
~Charles Kuralt

Bob Phillips – Texas Storyteller

Bob Phillips' influence extends beyond entertainment and the 50+ years of *Texas Country Reporter*. He has created a cultural archive that preserves the heart of Texas (and now the rest of the U.S) for future generations. His dedication to showcasing the stories of others while remaining humble himself aligns closely with the idea of living a "truly significant" life, one that lifts others up through genuine connection and storytelling.

As a curious soul, he would begin with a moment to listen, to care, to ask the question that unlocks a lifetime of memories or untold wisdom.

In this hurried age of scrolling and swiping, the art of storytelling —real, heartfelt storytelling—has become a rare treasure. It's the act of sitting still long enough to hear the unspoken, to see the invisible, to honor the dignity of every person, no matter how humble their station.

Bob Phillips understood this. Armed with little more than a microphone, a camera, and an insatiable curiosity, he ventured into the backroads, the kitchens, the workshops of small-town Texas. He wasn't looking for fame, fortune, or flash. No, Bob was after something far more valuable: the soul of a story.

He knew the secret—the one most overlook. That people don't just want to be heard. They need to be understood. And so, he asked the kinds of questions that felt less like an interview and more like a conversation with an old friend. He made the invisible visible, the ordinary extraordinary, and the forgotten unforgettable.

Here's a single example from Bob:

The creek may not have a name, but the ranch sure does. It's The Old Wilson Place—land soaked in history, sweat, and the kind of quiet dignity that only the Texas wind can understand. And this afternoon, on the coldest day of the year, third-generation rancher Weldon Wilson stands at the heart of it all, with a mind full of memories and a herd of cattle to move.

Oh, the bunkhouse? Well, it's no luxury lodge, but it means the world to Weldon. It's a boxcar, turned shelter, turned shrine—a gallery of relics that whisper the legacy of a family rooted in the land. There's his parents' old mailbox, his grandfather's walking cane, and a thousand stories etched in the dust on the windowsill. To someone else, it might look like junk. To Weldon, it's a lifeline.

"It's history," he says, with a sigh heavy enough to carry the weight of his grandpa's name. "And history's fading away."

165

But today isn't about fading away. Today is about holding on. It's about Weldon's herd of pure Texas Longhorn cattle, staring back at him with calm, knowing eyes. "They're friends," Weldon says, chuckling, and you'd believe him. Because in a world that feels like it's rushing toward tomorrow, these cattle are a living, breathing testament to yesterday.

Tomorrow, at sunrise, it begins—a cattle drive. Sixteen miles of Texas backroads, from pasture to pasture, with nine cowboys, seven horses, and one steadfast mule leading the way. Not for show. Not for spectacle. No, this is about business. Honest, old-fashioned, Texas-business.

"I want to get there," Weldon says, "with as many as I left with."

The morning is brisk, the sky painted in the hues of hope and tradition. The cowboys fan out, a living formation that seems to materialize straight from history books. Weldon mounts his mule, a 16-year-old veteran of these drives. Why a mule? Well, it's because his dad rode one. And in a quiet way, every step that mule takes honors the man who taught Weldon everything he knows.

The herd moves steadily, navigating dusty trails and county roads. But the moment of truth comes when they reach U.S. Highway 377—a strip of modernity slicing through tradition. Traffic halts, horns wait, and cowboys guide the Longhorns with an unspoken choreography passed down through generations.

It's tense. It's art. And when the last hoof crosses the asphalt, Weldon exhales—a long, deep breath of relief, pride, and gratitude. "The last time I did this," he recalls, "a woman pulled up beside me and said, 'This is the most awesome thing I've ever seen in my life.'"

And she was right.

Six hours later, with the sun dipping low and the air growing colder, Weldon looks back. The herd is safe. The cowboys are tired but smiling. And time? Well, for a moment, time itself stood still.

Weldon wipes a tear and nods when asked how long he'll keep doing this. "As long as I can," he whispers. Because for Weldon Wilson, this isn't just a cattle drive. It's a journey—of family, of tradition, of holding on to the things that matter.

And in those stories, there were lessons. About resilience and kindness. About dreams carved from nothing and communities stitched together with love. About the sacred dignity of a life lived simply, but well.

Bob's curiosity wasn't a fleeting thing—it was purposeful. It was the kind of curiosity that treats every person like a treasure chest waiting to be unlocked. He listened not to respond, but to truly hear. And when he told those stories, he didn't just tell them—he shared them, gifting them back to the world like a mirror reflecting our shared humanity.

So, as you navigate your day, pause. Look beyond the surface. Be curious—not nosy, but genuinely curious. Ask the kind of questions that don't just scratch the surface, but dig deep into the heart of a person. And then listen. Really listen. Because you just might find, in their story, the answer to a question you didn't know you were asking.

And that is the significance of great storytelling.

Listen to the entire conversation with Bob Phillips on *Success Made to Last* by scanning this QR code.

37

SIGNIFICANCE OF TRANSLATING THE TRUTH

God's marvelous grace imparts to each one of us varying gifts.
If your grace-gift is serving, then thrive in serving others well.
~Romans 12:6–7 TPT

Dr. Brian Simmons – Lead Translator, The Passion Translation Bible

Brian Simmons Ph.D. experienced what he describes as a supernatural encounter in 2009. This experience led to the development of *The Passion Translation* (TPT), a project aimed at expressing God's love and truth in contemporary language. TPT seeks to convey the emotion and life-changing essence of the Scriptures, merging the original biblical languages—Hebrew, Greek, and Aramaic—with modern English to resonate deeply with readers

Brian and Candice Simmons have been married for over 48 years. They are blessed with three children, six grandchildren, and three great-grandchildren. Their enduring commitment to faith and family continues to inspire many in their spiritual journey.

Visit www.thepassiontranslation.com

Throughout my life, there have been a chosen few—translators, if you will. Not just individuals who could interpret words, but those who could interpret meaning. They stood above teachers, professors, even chieftains. These were mentors—prized interpreters who understood history, context, and heart, and they could take something complex and distill it down so even a child could grasp it.

One such translator entered my life through an unlikely introduction. His name? Dr. Brian Simmons. And the connection? Carlton Garborg, founder of Broadstreet Publishing. The year was ... well, let's just say it was a moment in time destined by God. Carlton introduced me to *The Passion Translation Bible,* and I read a passage that didn't just speak to me—it resonated in my soul.

And that's how our lifelong mentorship with Brian began. Through Carlton, we connected with a man who wasn't just a scholar or a translator—he was a passionate lover of God. A man whose dramatic conversion to Christ in 1971 sparked a fire that has yet to dim. From the moment Brian gave his life to Jesus, he knew his calling: to bring the message of God's grace to those who had never heard it.

Brian and his wife, Candice, took that calling seriously. Together, they embarked on an extraordinary journey—packing up their three young children and moving to the tropical rainforests of Panama. For nearly eight years, they lived among the Paya-Kuna people, planting churches and working on a New Testament translation project. It was no small task. Brian had studied linguistics and Bible translation principles, equipping him to dive deep into the language, culture, and hearts of the people he served.

These two—Brian and Candice—have been described as pioneers in ministry. Their teaching, spiritual gifts, and genuine love for people have opened doors in nations around the world. For over four decades, they've dedicated themselves to presenting Christ in His fullness wherever God has sent them.

But there's more to this story. Brian isn't just a missionary or a linguist. He's the lead translator of *The Passion Translation*®—a heart-level rendering of the Bible that merges Hebrew, Greek, and Aramaic texts to express God's fiery love for this generation. It's not merely a translation of words; it's an interpretation of God's passion. It seeks to ignite an overwhelming response in readers, drawing them closer to the heart of God.

After their time in Panama, Brian and Candice returned to North America, planting dynamic ministries and founding Passion & Fire Ministries. They've traveled the globe, teaching and preaching the message of awakening and revival. Along the way, Brian authored countless books and devotionals that have helped readers encounter God's heart in fresh, life-changing ways.

And yet, it was *The Passion Translation* that opened God's Word to us in a new way. So much so, we began using it in *Gracefully Yours* greeting cards. One verse, in particular, became the cornerstone of our mission—Hebrews 10:25: "Discover creative ways to encourage others and to motivate them toward acts of compassion, doing beautiful works as expressions of love."

Of significance is this: Brian Simmons and his team of translators have done something groundbreaking. They've reintroduced the fire of the Bible to a world desperate for its warmth. In a time when God is often rejected and the church opposed, their work reminds us that while the message of God's Word is timeless, the methods by which it's communicated must resonate with the hearts of today's readers.

Enjoy the entire conversation with Dr. Brian Simmons on *Success Made to Last* podcast by scanning this QR code.

38

SIGNIFICANCE OF COURAGE

"I was saved for a purpose."

~General Earl Rudder

General Earl Rudder - D-Day hero,
President of Texas A&M University

General Earl Rudder led a truly significant life marked by extraordinary service, leadership, and lasting impact on Texas A&M University and the United States. Celebrated for his heroism during World War II, as a lieutenant colonel, he led the U.S. Army's 2nd Ranger Battalion during the D-Day invasion of Normandy on June 6, 1944. Despite suffering severe casualties, Rudder's courage and determination earned him the Distinguished Service Cross, Silver Star, and Purple Heart.

After the war, Rudder served as the mayor of Brady, Texas, demonstrating a dedication to community and civic service. His leadership extended to higher education when he became the President of Texas A&M University in 1959.

Earl Rudder's influence is still celebrated today. The Rudder Tower at Texas A&M and the Earl Rudder Freeway in Bryan-College Station stand as testaments to his impact. His courage, integrity, and vision embody the essence of a life lived for the betterment of others.

Earl Rudder, the quiet Texan with the steely gaze, was born to a world of flat plains and boundless skies in Eden, Texas. His story, though, reaches far beyond that humble beginning.

It was the 6th of June, 1944. D-Day. Normandy. A day when the free world stood on the brink, teetering between tyranny and liberation. And standing on Omaha Beach, with 225 Rangers under his command, was Lt. Colonel Earl Rudder. Their mission? To scale the 100-foot cliffs of Pointe du Hoc under a rain of fire and fury.

The odds? Grim. The stakes? Unimaginable.

But Rudder didn't flinch. He didn't waver. Leading from the front, he inspired his men with a quiet determination, the kind you couldn't fake. Those men climbed, clawed, and bled their way up those cliffs, silencing the German guns that threatened thousands of lives below. Two-thirds of his men fell that day. And yet, they succeeded. Why? Because Rudder led with his heart, his grit, and a sense of duty larger than himself.

But the story doesn't end on those cliffs.

Earl Rudder's battlefield leadership was just a chapter in his tale. When the war ended, Rudder came home—not to rest, but to rebuild. A soldier, yes, but also a teacher, he turned his attention to shaping the future.

By 1959, he was named President of Texas A&M University. At the time, A&M was a struggling military school, isolated in tradition, shrinking in relevance. It was said that the university's future looked as bleak as those cliffs at Normandy. But Earl Rudder? He saw potential.

He opened the doors to women, integrated the campus, and transformed A&M into a modern institution—one where the Corps of Cadets and civilian students could learn side by side. His reforms weren't always popular. In fact, some said they felt like a storm. But Rudder knew that true leadership wasn't about being liked; it was about doing what was right.

And so, just as he had climbed Pointe du Hoc to clear the path for freedom, he scaled the walls of resistance to clear the path for progress.

By the time he passed in 1970, Earl Rudder had left a legacy on two battlefields—the beaches of Normandy and the grounds of Aggieland. Today, his name is etched into the history books, the hearts of Aggies, and the cliffs of Normandy. In a fitting celebration of the General, Rudder Tower stands 110 feet tall, the exact height of the cliffs of Pointe du Hoc.

Listen to our dedication to General Earl Rudder on *Success Made to Last* podcast by scanning this QR code.

By the way, I proposed to my wife in Rudder Tower back in 1979.

39

SIGNIFICANCE OF MULTIPLYING THE MULTIPLIERS

"See the world, make a difference."

~Deb Kielty

Deb Kielty and the P&G Alumni Foundation

Deb Kielty, P&G Alumni Foundation Chairwoman, shares her personal journey of significance and provides insight on how the P&G Alumni Foundation changes and improves lives.

Established in 2001, the P&G Alumni Network was formed to help P&G Alums across the globe stay connected.

Today, the Network has grown to 35,000+ Alumni strong and is a premier membership organization delivering against three strategic pillars:

- Engagement facilitates connections and networking through chapter activities, the global conferences and the Women's Leadership Forum.
- Enrichment offers additional ways for Alumni to connect regarding thought leadership, best practices, training, and development.
- Philanthropy affords P&G Alumni to "give back" personally or within their chapters and is also achieved through the P&G Alumni Foundation, the Network's charitable arm.

Visit www.pgalumnifoundation.org

A remarkable journey often speaks to the heart of finding significance in our world sooner rather than later.
"See the world. Make a difference."

These six profound words, inspired by Deb Kielty's mother, became the guiding star in Deb's life. At the tender age of 17, during a Spanish Club trip to Mexico, Deb first glimpsed life beyond the borders of the United States. This journey opened her eyes to a world where inequities abounded, and where she felt a deep calling to contribute meaningfully.

During her travels, Deb tracked her four-week adventure on a detailed map of Mexico. It wasn't a luxurious journey; there were no flights or plush hotels. Instead, it was an experience grounded in reality—backpacks, buses, and a Spanish teacher as their guide. Upon returning home, Deb presented her mother with her ripped and crumpled map, sharing how the world had unfolded before her eyes. Her mother, a dedicated social worker and champion for the marginalized, reciprocated by gifting her a map of the world.

Deb realized then that her curiosity and belief in her potential, despite modest beginnings, would fuel her quest to see the world and make a difference. She sought ways to have others sponsor her journey to significance, considering avenues like the Peace Corps and the United States Information Agency. Her academic pursuits in Spanish, international relations, and bilingual education were steps toward her goal. An interview with Pan American Airlines seemed like a promising start, but a hiring freeze halted her plans. Undeterred, Deb returned to academia, earning a Master's in International Management. This led her to Procter & Gamble (P&G), where her career would allow her to fulfill her early North Star vision.

At P&G, Deb found her ideal company, where she could work and fulfill what her mom had inspired—"to change lives." Deb quickly learned the profound impact one could have on others. Her first international assignment in Mexico with P&G, just two years into her tenure, revealed how she could influence young leaders across sectors. As she ascended the organizational ladder, she became a role model for many, particularly women leaders in regions like Asia and Europe, where female representation at decision-making tables was scarce.

Exposure to Stephen Covey's principles, particularly the concept of the sphere of influence, reinforced Deb's belief in her ability to bring more women into influential roles. As Vice President of Worldwide Strategic Planning, she leveraged her position to champion diversity and inclusion. Later, as President of the World Trade Center Institute (WTCI), Deb co-founded the annual Women Spanning the Globe Leadership Conference, now in its 20th year.

Cross-Generational Significance

Deb observes a commendable mindfulness in today's younger generation regarding what truly matters. Despite sometimes receiving a bad rap, this generation aspires to significance in their work and daily activities. Deb sees this firsthand with two daughters in their 20s, and WTCI's Youth Diplomats program. The younger generation possess technological tools and social media platforms to really amplify their impact. To harness this energy, Deb is currently collaborating with WTCI to develop and launch a multi-generational mentoring program, blending wisdom from experienced professionals with the vigor of younger minds. This fellowship program will serve as an energizing forum where students, mid-career leaders, and retired executives exchange life stories and learn from one another—enabling younger generations and seniors to achieve even greater impact across meaningful endeavors.

Stephen Covey's concept of the sphere of influence resonates deeply with Deb and the P&G Alumni Foundation. To be significant, one must view the glass as half full and work with diverse groups to make an impact. For Deb, the P&G alumni, numbering more than 100,000, represent a vast sphere of influence. WTCI, with its extensive mid-Atlantic and global reach, adds to this formidable network.

The Secret to the P&G Foundation's Success

Founded in 2003, the P&G Alumni Network aimed to connect the talent, ideas, and resources of P&G alumni. Philanthropy has been a key tenet since inception, with the Network supporting various causes. In 2013, the establishment of the P&G Alumni Foundation, a 501(c)(3) organization, formalized these efforts, with a focus on fundraising and global grant-making to non-profits where P&G alumni are actively involved. The foundation's mission, inspired by P&G's core values—integrity, trust, leadership, and a passion for winning—aims to address societal inequities.

As Dr. Janet B. Reid, a P&G alum and board member, noted, the foundation's real strength lies in its multiplying effect, leveraging the scale and expertise of P&G alumni around the world.

The foundation's success hinges on P&G alumni involvement and its rigorous grant selection process. Every grant requires a P&G Alumni Grant Champion, someone who has collaborated with the applying nonprofit for at least a year and can vouch for its potential impact. This process, coupled with the competitive spirit of P&G alumni, ensures that the best initiatives receive support.

If you, your community or corporation are forming a foundation, adopting the Grant Champion will be a critical element, guiding dollars to the right people to change lives. This "boots on the ground" will allow you to inspect what you expect.

The stories of P&G alums Mike Kremzar and Arlene Golembiewski exemplify the foundation's impact. Mike started the Cincinnati Cooks program, a workforce development initiative within the Freestore Foodbank. This program not only trains individuals for food service jobs but also uses the food prepared during training to feed the hungry. As a P&G Alumni Foundation grant recipient, Cincinnati Cooks credits the foundation's early support with their ability to raise nearly three times as much in other donations. Under Mike's leadership, and with the involvement of fifteen other P&G alums, this program has flourished.

Arlene, a former Peace Corps volunteer, founded the Sherbro Foundation in Sierra Leone. With P&G Alumni Foundation's support, she expanded employment opportunities and introduced computer literacy in a rural village. This initiative, supported by grants from organizations like Rotary International, has helped transform lives, including that of Sulaiman Timbo, who is now completing an MBA and launching new programs in remote villages. According to Arlene "the first P&G Alumni Foundation grant was our catalyst, inspiring Rotary Club to take a risk with us. Since then, we have increased five times the number and scale of our projects."

The foundation's ripple effect is vast. Alumni involvement in various initiatives leads to matching grants, in-kind donations, and synergies with other organizations. For instance, a grant recipient working on job readiness and computer center programs for orphans in Africa leveraged the P&G Alumni Foundation's support to secure government assistance for solar panels. This more affordable source of power helped to extend the operating hours of the computer center, with more people gaining access and training.

The foundation's multipliers are impressive. With over 125 P&G Alumni Foundation grants now impacting people in need across 42 countries, the multipliers and ripple effects are growing exponentially. In the spirit of Stephen Covey's principle of an abundance mentality, The P&G Alumni Foundation's approach offers a blueprint for others to accelerate their journey to significance. By taking the relevant learning from this model, organizations and communities can make a meaningful difference sooner.

More people now aspire to make a difference, whether by seeing the world or by impacting their immediate surroundings. The key is to pursue significance each day, fueled by passion and guided by principle-centered leadership.

The ripple effect of Deb's work and the foundation's initiatives are evident in the diverse thinkers and P&G alumni local champions making a tangible difference in individuals' lives. By identifying and nurturing spheres of influence, and trusting in their power, we can collectively create a greater impact. As Deb concludes, "We are uniquely blessed with values that bind us together to serve and change lives. Consider your own spheres of influence, the journey of others to significance, and watch how you, too, can change lives." And when you reach significance, share your formula with the world so the multiplying effect can perpetuate.

Enjoy more of the story on *Success Made to Last* podcast by scanning this QR code.

40

SIGNIFICANCE OF IGNITING OTHERS

"Together we can. Together we will. Together we must change the world."

~Dr. Jane Goodall

Dr. Jane Goodall - Founder, The Jane Goodall Institute,
UN Messenger of Peace

Jane Goodall, Ph.D. and Ethologist, is the founder of the Jane Goodall Institute, a United Nations Messenger of Peace and Dame Commander of the Most Excellent Order of the British Empire. Jane's study of animal behavior has contributed to the branch of knowledge called ethology, the study of behavior. She is best known for her exceptionally detailed and long-term research on the chimpanzees of Gombe National Park in Tanzania which began in 1960.

In 1977, she co-founded the Jane Goodall Institute for Wildlife Research, Education and Conservation. (JGI). JGI's method of community-centered conservation is now active in 6 African countries.

In 1991, the Jane Goodall "Roots & Shoots" humanitarian and environmental program for young people was founded. Young people of all ages are empowered to choose and become involved in hands on programs benefitting people, animals and the environment.

In 2002, Jane Goodall was appointed United Nations Messenger of Peace.

Visit www.janegoodall.org

In a quiet English town called Bournemouth, a young girl named Jane found her passion for animals both in books and in the backyard.

At the age of five when visiting family friends, Jane Goodall hid in a hen house to learn about chickens and how they laid their eggs.

Fast forward to 1960. A determined Jane arrived at the Gombe in western Tanzania with nothing but a notebook, binoculars, and an unshakable belief that she could unravel the mysteries of the animal kingdom. You see, at that time, women didn't venture into the jungles of Africa to study wild animals. But Jane wasn't just any woman.

She sat. And she watched. Day after day. Month after month. Her patience and persistence paid off when she made a discovery that would upend everything we thought we knew about our closest relatives: chimpanzees made and used tools. For years, humanity had clung to the belief that tool-making was the exclusive domain of human animals. But there they were—chimpanzees, stripping leaves from twigs to fish termites from mounds. Jane proved what many scientists refused to believe—chimpanzees were more like us than we ever dared to imagine.

Her work didn't stop with the science. She gave her chimpanzees names—David Greybeard, Flo, and Fifi—because to Jane, they weren't just subjects of research. They were individuals with emotions, relationships, and personalities. A radical notion at the time, but one that made the world take a second look at its kinship with the animal kingdom.

Then the story takes a different turn. In 1986 Jane saw the forests where her chimpanzees lived begin to disappear. She saw communities struggling in poverty, forced to encroach on habitats just to survive. She realized that if she wanted to save the chimps, she'd have to save the people, too.

And so, Jane Goodall became more than a scientist. She became a conservationist.

In 1991, she launched Jane Goodall's Roots & Shoots, a

program to empower young people of all ages to become involved in hands-on projects of their choosing to benefit the community, animals (including domestic animals), and the environment. Roots & Shoots is now active in more than 75 countries.

One of its shining moments came in Flint, Michigan, during the water crisis. A group of students took action, distributing clean water and planting community gardens. Their efforts gave their neighbors hope—and reminded us all of the power of young minds to change the world.

Then followed the TACARE project, and Dr. Jane and the Jane Goodall Institute launched initiatives that helped local communities adopt sustainable practices—like agroforestry and clean water programs—that not only lifted people out of poverty but allowed them to become partners in conserving their heritage and also preserved the forests her beloved chimps called home.

One village at a time, one program at a time, Jane showed the world that conservation isn't just about saving animals. It's about saving ourselves.

Today, Dr. Jane Goodall is a household name. She's traveled millions of miles, spoken to millions of people, and inspired countless individuals to join her crusade for a better planet. She's been knighted, honored with awards, and was appointed by Secretary General Kofi Annan as a UN Messenger of Peace. But she'll tell you her most significant accomplishment isn't a title or a trophy. It's the spark she's ignited in others—a spark of hope, of empathy, of responsibility.

Jane Goodall's story isn't just about chimps or science or even conservation. It's about the courage to follow your curiosity, the humility to recognize the interconnectedness of all life, and the determination to leave the world a better place than you found it.

Enjoy this interview on *Success Made to Last* network featuring Tim Love on *Discovering Truth with Dr. Jane Goodall* by scanning this QR code.

41

SIGNIFICANCE OF STAYING TRUE TO THE SOIL

*"The true measure of a man's worth is not found in the title
he holds, but in the land he tends, the people he serves, and the
promises he keeps when no one is watching."*
~Truly Significant Texan Podcast

Texas Department of Agriculture Commissioner Sid Miller

In the long, unbroken chronicle of American public life, every now and then you meet a figure who seems carved not from marble, but from earth. Soil under the fingernails. Sun on the neck. Wind in the face. The kind of person whose story starts long before any title ever lands on a desk.

Sid Miller is one of those stories.

You may know him as the Texas Commissioner of Agriculture.

Picture the familiar white hat—the look of a man who still carries the dust and dignity of rural Texas with him into every room he enters.

But what you may not know, at least not until now, is the deeper truth. The one we call true significance. A life measured not by applause, nor authority, but by endurance, service, sacrifice, and the steady moral compass that points a person toward others, not toward themselves.

Sid Miller entered this world on September 6, 1955. He was the second of five children born to Dean and Charlene Miller. His father was a rancher of the old American mold. His mother was a homemaker, teacher, and quiet force whose lessons filled both the classroom and the kitchen table.

Life on that farm was not romantic. It was real.

Sheep. Goats. Hogs. Cattle. Peanuts. Grain sorghum. Hay stacked high in the summer sun.

Sid's early resume? Milking cows at dawn, gathering eggs at dusk, butchering hogs, hauling hay, fishing creek banks, and shooting squirrels for supper. Transportation? A pet sheep, then a donkey pulling a little cart, and only after years of bareback riding, finally, a saddle.

He would later say that long wait made him a better horseman, and eventually a champion rodeo cowboy.

Life was full, but it was not easy.

One spring, a hailstorm cracked open the sky. Grapefruit-sized stones hammered the land.

Hundreds of newly sheared goats were lost. A young Sid watched nature give and take in the same breath and learned the resilience that ranch families hold deep in their bones.

His father had simple measures for a good day:

Up before dawn. Coffee at the café. News traded over Formica tables. Then home to saddle a horse and move cattle before the heat arrived with help from his dogs.

The Millers' border collies could gather twenty head of cattle into a trailer from the brush with no more than a whistle. They were worth four or five good men.

But life tested them with forces harsher than weather.

The Year Everything Changed—1974

President Nixon froze beef prices. The timing was fatal. Sid's father had cattle on every lease he could find. When the government froze prices, the bottom dropped out. The Millers lost everything—land, savings, even Sid's mother's car.

And then came the accident. His father, the tough Marine, was thrown from a horse.

A traumatic brain injury was followed by a year-long coma in a VA hospital.

The family survived, but nothing looked the same.

Sid himself was a senior in high school, his leg broken from bull riding. He couldn't work. His mother, with three kids at home, took a minimum-wage job.

College dreams? All but gone until a mentor, an agriculture teacher made one phone call.

And the boy with B grades and a work ethic bigger than Texas earned an academic scholarship to Cisco Junior College.

One act of belief. One door cracked open. One life forever changed.

His leg healed. A rodeo scholarship followed. Tarleton State University came next.

And so did marriage. Sid and Debra were just two kids working their way through school. Sid shoeing horses and working the sale barn. Debra working at Safeway. She finished college in three and a half years. He in four.

And Sid Miller became an agriculture teacher, the calling he had heard as a boy.

Five years. $9,600 annual salary. A growing family.

And so, he stepped into business, first digging up trees to sell, then buying a nursery in Stephenville, Texas in 1985.

The economy collapsed. By every rule of logic, that nursery should have folded. But Sid Miller does not fold.

He held on by grit. By faith. By stubborn determination wrapped in old-school Texas resolve.

And then, public service found him.

He was recruited to run for the Texas House. This was a seat Republicans hadn't won since the Civil War. Sid and Debra knocked on 12,000 doors. No political pedigree or experience.

They were just two working-class Texans who believed the people deserved a voice that sounded like them.

And they won. Twelve years in the Texas House. Then the call to run for Commissioner of Agriculture.

He won again, three terms and counting.

All while running cattle, horses, and a nursery that remains rooted in the soil of Stephenville.

But if you ask Sid Miller who the real hero of the family is he will point to his wife Debra.

A teacher. A counselor. A warrior for young people the world had overlooked.

One day she walked in the door and said she had resigned. Not burned out. Not worn down, but called to create an alternative high school. Debra wanted to go to work for teen mothers, for kids fighting addiction, for youth with trauma, language barriers, and for those from broken homes.

"We'll give them a shot at the American Dream," Debra said. And she did. For twenty years.

Later, she opened another school in a residential treatment center. The students were guaranteed to attend. Hope was no longer an elective.

And Sid will tell you the truth plainly:

"She serves because she is godly. She sees the unseen. She acts when others hesitate."

That's the built in role model that Commissioner Sid Miller has in the family. Debra is what true significance looks like.

The Steward of Texas Agriculture

True significance is rarely loud in government. It shows up quietly in balanced books, cleared backlogs, and in farmers who can keep farming.

Under Sid Miller's watch as Texas Agriculture Commissioner, the Texas Department of Agriculture was not merely managed, it was restored. An agency carrying an $18 million deficit was transformed into a balanced, efficient operation—one singularly focused on strengthening Texas agriculture and serving those who depend on it. Within just six months of his first term, Miller eliminated a 2½-year backlog in organic certifications, restoring trust, timeliness, and opportunity for Texas producers.

But stewardship is more than repair, it is foresight. Miller revitalized the State of Texas Agricultural Relief (STAR) Fund, securing $1.3 million in private donations to help agricultural communities recover when disaster strikes. He established the TDA Office of Water Policy, ensuring agriculture has a seat at the table in state water planning. And through the Farm Fresh Initiative, he connected Texas farmers directly with Texas schools—delivering more than $300 million worth of locally sourced, healthy meals to students across the state while strengthening local economies.

Significance also understands that Texas agriculture does not stop at the state line. Committed to global trade, Commissioner Miller has traveled to every continent except Antarctica, opening and expanding markets for Texas-grown products. At home, he improved operational efficiency by reducing inspector travel by 1.5 million miles, launched Operation Maverick to strengthen consumer protection, and increased fuel pump inspections from once every twelve years to every year, protecting both farmers and families.

Under his leadership, regulatory subsidies were cut by 50 percent, shifting the department to full cost recovery. Costly contracts were canceled. Operations went paperless. Taxpayer dollars were saved, not by retreating from responsibility, but by honoring it while agriculture and consumer safeguards were reinforced.

Sid Miller did not simply oversee a department. He mobilized a movement—rooted in heritage, strengthened by innovation, and committed to defending the future of the Texas farmer.

Because he understands a lasting truth: Significance is not found in the white hat you wear, but in the people you serve.

Legacy Beyond Titles

And now, as the fourth term as Commissioner approaches, he leads, rides and works like a man twenty years younger, ever invigorated by the opportunity to build a stronger Texas agricultural economy. His legacy is less important than the lives Sid Miller has lifted.

The rancher's kids who stayed on the land because someone fought for their future.

The students who found hope in the classrooms his wife built.

The rural communities revived by vision and courage.

The young Texans who now see agriculture not as a relic...but as a calling.

They may never know his name, but they will feel his impact. Because Sid Miller has lived a life not of fame, but of true significance. And his beloved State of Texas is better because of it.

Enjoy this bonus narrative on Commissioner Sid Miller from our *Truly Significant* podcast by scanning this QR code.

EPILOGUE

I hope that you have enjoyed this journey through *Truly Significant: Conversations with Big Hearted People.* It is more than a book—it is a collection of stories from ordinary people who experienced extraordinary transformations. These are not tales of wealth or fame, but of lives changed, hearts opened, and communities uplifted.

Each story reminds us of the incredible power of choice—the choice to live with purpose, to align our actions with values that matter, and to leave a legacy of hope. Kindness, generosity, and philanthropy aren't just lofty ideals. They're the tools that build bridges, the sparks that light dark corners, and the actions that transform intentions into impact.

As you close this book, reflect on what your story might say. Not about your possessions or accomplishments, but about the lives you have touched and the love you shared. Imagine this: your final check bounces—not because you miscalculated, but because you gave all you had. What remains is not the wealth you accumulated, but the legacy of significance you left behind.

Writing this final page, I am reminded of a quote by Ralph Waldo Emerson. "Our advances are not made by gradation, such as can be represented by motion in a straight line, by rather by ascension of state."

Consider your ascension into significance as a new plateau. Taking just one step toward another person in need, is a step of significance. You have left "me" for "we." And read this carefully. Your legacy doesn't have to bolster your ego with a name of a college building, but rather a simple expression of generosity.

So go ahead. Rethink your legacy. Write it every day with acts of kindness. And when the time comes, may your final act of giving resonate louder than any thank-you ever could. That's the power of significance.

Personalized Life Purpose & Giving Back Assessment Worksheet

Section 1: Core Values & Life Themes

Instructions: Reflect on and answer the following:

* What significant core values have consistently guided your decisions?
  (e.g., compassion, wisdom, legacy, faith, justice)
  ➤ My core values are:
* Who inspired you to live a life of service? What traits did they model?
  ➤ One person who inspired me was... They showed me...
* In moments of joy or clarity, what were you doing? Were you alone or helping others?
  ➤ When I feel most alive, I am...

Section 2: Time, Talent, and Treasure Inventory

Instructions: Identify what you currently offer the world.

Domain	Current Contributions	Future Aspirations
Time	(e.g., mentoring, volunteering)	(e.g., increase mentorship hours)
Talent	(e.g., writing, teaching, coaching)	(e.g., teach podcasting to youth)
Treasure	(e.g., giving to causes, funding art)	(e.g., start a giving foundation)

Section 3: Truly Significant Reflection Questions

Instructions: Free-write your answers in full paragraphs.

1. **What legacy do I want to leave behind?**
2. **How do I define "a truly significant life well lived"?**
3. **If I had one year left to live, what would I focus on?**
4. **What breaks my heart—and can I help change it?**
5. **Whose lives have I changed already, and how?**

Section 4: The Ikigai Map (Purpose Intersection)

Use this to identify overlap in your life purpose.

Ikigai Question	Your Answer
What do I love?	(e.g., storytelling, connecting with others)
What am I good at?	(e.g., writing, inspiring, mentoring)
What does the world need from me?	(e.g., guidance, compassion, truth-telling)
What can I be paid for / sustain myself on?	(e.g., books, programs, consulting)

➤ If "what the world needs" includes healing, hope, or connection, your purpose likely involves giving back.

Section 5: Diagnostic Scorecard

Rate each on a scale of 1–5 (1 = not at all, 5 = completely):

- I feel most fulfilled when I help others grow or heal
- My talents are best used in service to people, not just business goals
- Giving (time, money, gifts) brings me deep joy
- I often seek to create legacy, not just success
- My spiritual beliefs encourage generosity and humility
- I feel called to build or support something bigger than myself

Total Score Interpretation:

- **24–30:** Your life purpose is strongly rooted in giving back.
- **18–23:** Giving is likely a core element; explore this further.
- **Below 18:** You may have multiple callings of significance—service may be one, but not central.

Section 6: Action Planning

Top 3 Ways I Can Give Back Starting This Month:
1.
2.
3.
People I Can Mentor or Support Now:
➤
Organizations or Causes I Could Partner With:
➤

NOTES

Chapter 1. *The Spare Room* © 2021 by Emily Chang, New York, Post Hill Press; www.MyShanghai.org.

Chapter 2. *The One Minute Manager* ©1982 by Dr. Ken Blanchard and Spencer Johnson. New York, Morrow.

Chapter 3. *Five Love Languages* © 1992 by Dr. Gary Chapman, Chicago, Northfield Publishing.

Chapter 4. www.poachconsulting.com, 2025

Chapter 5. *Radical Candor* © 2017 by Kim Scott, New York, St. Martin's Press.

Chapter 6. www.gatewaychurch.com

Chapter 7. *The Respect Dare* © 2012, by Nina Roesner, Nashville, Tennessee, Thomas Nelson, Inc.

Chapter 8. *Berenstain Bears* © 1962 and Various Years, New York, Random House.

Chapter 9. Recorded in www.successmadetolast.com 2014 with 4 Word Women.

Chapter 10. *Man's Search for Meaning* © 1946 by Viktor Frankl, by Viktor Frankl, Vienna, Austria.

Chapter 11. *The Mind of God* © 2018 by Dr. Jay Lombard, New York, Penguin Random House.

Chapter 12. www.worldfoodbank.org

Chapter 13. *When Core Values are Strategic* © 2012 by Rick Tocquigny, New York, FT Press.

Chapter 14. www.successmadetolast.com 2024, Reunion Series.

Chapter 15. www.habitatforhumanity.org

Chapter 16. International Women's Coffee Alliance, 2025. www.womenincoffee.org

Chapter 17. www.stpaultaylor.com

Chapter 18. Inspired from *The Autobiography of Andrew Carnegie and the Gospel of Wealth*, © 1889, New York, Carnegie Corporation.

Chapter 19. www.coloradoEPIC.org, www.aclboulder.org, www.ymcanoco.org

Chapter 20. www.successmadetolast.com 2012, 2024 interviews.

Chapter 21. www.successmadetolast.com 2016 interview.

Chapter 22. *When Core Values are Strategic* © 2012 by Rick Tocquigny, New York, FT Press.

Chapter 23. *The Global Soul* © 2000, by Pico Iyer, New York, Vintage Departures.

Chapter 24. www.successmadetolast.com, 2020.

Chapter 25. *Elf on the Shelf* © 2005 by Chanda Bell and Carol Aebersold, New York, Self Published. www.elfontheshelf.com, www.luminstella.com

Chapter 26. www.successmadetolast.com 2024, Reunion Series.

Chapter 27. *Significance Newsletter* © 2024 by Rick Tocquigny. www.promisekeepers.org

Chapter 28. www.teammates.org. 1991

Chapter 29. www.successmadetolast.com 2024

Chapter 30. www.solight-designs.com

Chapter 31 www.hbs.edu/faculty/Pages/profile.aspx?facId=6476

Chapter 32. *Significance Newsletter* © 2019 by Rick Tocquigny.

Chapter 33. www.successmadetolast.com, 2015.

Chapter 34. www.successmadetolast.com, 2011.

Chapter 35. *Walking With Gorillas* © 2023 by Gladys Kalema-Zikusoka, New York Arcade Publishing, www.CTPH.org

Chapter 36. www.successmadetolast.com 2023. www.crossroadstoday.com.

Chapter 37. *The Passion Translation Bible* ® © 2014, Translated directly from the original Hebrew text by Dr. Brian Simmons, Racine, Wisconsin, Broadstreet Publishing.

Chapter 38. *Significance Newsletter* © 2024 by Rick Tocquigny

Chapter 39. Procter and Gamble Alumni Foundation, 2024, www.pgalums.com/give-back/ #donate.

Chapter 40. *Discovering Truth* © 2022 by Tim Love, New York, Internationalist Press.

Rick Tocquigny – Author, Podcaster, Mentor

Rick Tocquigny is on an odyssey to understand the scope and value of serving others. His Austin, Texas-based company, Success Made to Last Media, www.successmadetolast.com, features divisions devoted to publishing, podcasting and mentoring start ups. Each division has a give back component to create a social-legacy.

Rick gained invaluable experience from his careers at P&G, Frito-Lay, and General Mills. Now in his 16th year in podcasting, his team has produced over 4,000 shows, interviewing people whose work and volunteering can be called significant. He is the award winning author of *When Core Values are Strategic*, published in three languages, *Life Lessons from Veterans*, *Life Lessons from Family Vacations*, four other *Life Lessons* books, along with *Gracefully-Yours* greeting cards.

A graduate of Texas A&M University, Rick and Carla, his wife of more than 45 years, have two daughters and two grandchildren... the source of his deepest joy. And now, they take drum lessons from their Papa Rico learning all the Aggie cadences.

Stay in touch with Rick by visiting www.trulysignificant.com.

Enjoy more fine books from WordCrafts Press by visiting www.wordcrafts.net or by scanning this QR code.

For bulk order discounts for corporate events, communities, leadership, employees and volunteers, please contact sales@wordcrafts.net.